CHANGE OR DIE

ALSO BY ALAN DEUTSCHMAN

A Tale of Two Valleys: Wine, Wealth, and
   the Battle for the Good Life in Napa and Sonoma

The Second Coming of Steve Jobs

CHANGE OR DIE

*The Three Keys to Change
at Work and in Life*

Alan Deutschman

HARPER

NEW YORK · LONDON · TORONTO · SYDNEY

HARPER

A hardcover edition of this book was published in 2007 by Regan, an imprint of HarperCollins Publishers.

HarperCollins books may be purchased for educational, business, or sales promotional use. For information please write: Special Markets Department, HarperCollins Publishers, 10 East 53rd Street, New York, NY 10022.

First Collins paperback edition published 2008

Designed by Jaime Putorti

Library of Congress Cataloging-in-Publication Data

Deutschman, Alan, 1965–
    Change or die : the three keys to change at work and in life / Alan Deutschman. —1st ed.
        xi, 241 p. ; 24 cm.
    Includes bibliographical references (p. 219–228) and index.
    Summary: "Journalist Deutschman has concluded that although we all have the ability to change our behavior, we rarely ever do. In fact, the odds are nine to one that, when faced with the dire, life-or-death need to change, we won't. From patients suffering from heart disease to repeat offenders in the criminal justice system to companies trapped in the mold of unsuccessful business practices, many of us could prevent ominous outcomes by simply changing our mindset. This book debunks age-old myths about change and empowers us with three critical keys—relate, repeat, and reframe—to help us make important positive changes in our lives. It's not about merely reorganizing or restructuring our priorities—it's about challenging, inspiring, and helping all of us to make the dramatic transformations necessary in any aspect of life, changes that are positive, attainable, and absolutely vital. —From publisher description." —from source other than the Library of Congress
        ISBN-13: 978-0-06-137367-1
    1. Change (Psychology) I. Title.
        [DNLM: 1. Adaptation, Psychological. 2. Behavior. 3. Health Behavior. 4. Organizational Innovation.]
        BF637.C4D48 2007
        155.2'4—dc22
                                                                        2006050442

        10 11 12 ID/RRD 10 9 8 7 6

To Susan

Contents

The Nine "Psych Concepts" of Change

INTRODUCTION

The Three Keys to Change

Change or die.

What if you were given that choice? *For real.* What if it weren't just the hyperbolic rhetoric that conflates corporate performance with life or death? Not the overblown exhortations of a rabid boss, or a maniacal coach, or a slick motivational speaker, or a self-dramatizing chief executive officer or political leader. We're talking actual life and death now. Your own life and death. What if a well-informed, trusted authority figure said you had to make difficult and enduring changes in the way you think, feel, and act? If you didn't, your time would end soon—a lot sooner than it had to. Could you change when change really mattered? When it mattered most?

Yes, you say?

Try again.

Yes?

You're probably deluding yourself.

That's what the experts say.

They say that you wouldn't change.

Don't believe it? You want odds? Here are the odds that the experts are laying down, their scientifically studied odds: nine to one. That's nine to one against you. How do you like those odds?

This revelation unnerved me when I heard it in November 2004 at a private conference at Rockefeller University, an elite medical research center in New York City. The event was hosted by the top executives at IBM, who invited the most brilliant thinkers they knew from around the world to come together for a day and propose solutions to some of the world's biggest problems. Their first topic was the crisis in health care, an industry that consumes an astonishing $2.1 trillion a year in the United States alone—more than one seventh of the entire economy. Despite all that spending, we're not feeling healthier, and we aren't making enough progress toward preventing the illnesses that kill us, such as heart disease, stroke, and cancer.

A dream team of experts took the stage, and you might have expected them to proclaim that breathtaking advances in science and technology—mapping the human genome and all that—held the long-awaited answers.

That's not what they said.

Speaking to the small group of insiders, they were unsparingly candid. They said that the cause of the health care crisis hadn't changed for decades, and the medical establishment still couldn't figure out what to do about it.

Dr. Raphael "Ray" Levey, founder of the Global Medical Forum, an annual summit meeting of leaders from every part of the health care system, told the audience: "A relatively small percentage of the population consumes the vast majority of the health care budget for diseases that are very well known and by and large behavioral." That is, they're sick because of how they choose to lead their lives, not because of factors beyond their control, such as the genes they were born with. Levey continued: "Even as far back as when I was in medical school"—he enrolled at Harvard in 1955—"many articles demonstrated that eighty percent of the health care budget was consumed by five behavioral issues." He didn't bother to name them, but you don't need an MD to guess what he was talking about: Too much smoking, drinking, and eating. Too much stress. Not enough exercise.

Then the really shocking news was presented by Dr. Edward Miller, dean of the medical school and chief executive officer of the hospital at Johns Hopkins University. He talked about patients whose arteries are so clogged that any kind of exertion is terribly painful for them. It hurts too much to take a long walk. It hurts too much to make love. So surgeons have to implant pieces of plastic to prop open their arteries, or remove veins from their legs to stitch near the heart so the blood can bypass the blocked passages. The procedures are traumatic and expensive—they can cost more than $100,000. More than one and a half million people every year in the United States undergo coronary bypass graft or angioplasty surgery at a total price of around $60 billion. Although these surgeries are astonishing feats, they are no more than temporary fixes. The operations relieve the patients' pain, at least for a while, but only rarely—fewer than 3 percent of the cases—prevent the heart attacks they're heading toward or prolong their lives. The bypass grafts often clog up within a few years; the angioplasties, in only a few months.

Knowing these grim statistics, doctors tell their patients: If you want to keep the pain from coming back, and if you don't want to have to repeat the surgery, and if you want to stop the course of your heart disease before it kills you, then you have to switch to a healthier lifestyle. You have to stop smoking, stop drinking, stop overeating, start exercising, and relieve your stress.

But very few do.

"If you look at people after coronary-artery bypass grafting two years later, ninety percent of them have not changed their lifestyle," Miller said. "And that's been studied over and over and over again. And so we're missing some link in there. Even though they know they have a very bad disease and they know they should change their lifestyle, for whatever reason, they can't."

That's been studied *over and over and over again*. The dean of the nation's most famous medical school said so with confidence. But following the conference, when I searched through the archives of the leading scientific journals, I came across something strange. Something that just didn't fit. In 1993, Dr. Dean Ornish, a professor of medicine at the University of California at San Francisco, convinced the Mutual of Omaha insurance company to pay for an unusual experiment. The researchers recruited 194 patients who suffered from severely clogged arteries and could have bypass grafts or angioplasties covered by their insurance plans. Instead they signed up for a trial. The staffers helped them quit smoking and switch to an extreme vegetarian diet that derived fewer than 10 percent of its calories from fat. In places like Omaha, they shifted from steaks and fries to brown rice and greens. The patients got together for group conversations twice a week, and they also took classes in meditation, relaxation, yoga, and aerobic exercise, which became parts of their daily routines.

The program lasted for only a year. After that, they were on their own. But three years from the start, the study found, 77 percent of the patients had stuck with these lifestyle changes—and safely avoided the need for heart surgery. They had halted—or, in many cases, reversed—the progress of their disease.

If the medical establishment was resigned to the supposed fact that only one out of every ten people can change, even in a crisis, then how did Dr. Ornish's team inspire and motivate nearly eight out of ten of its heart patients to accomplish and sustain such dramatic transformations?

•

In 2002 the Justice Department published a study that tracked 272,111 inmates after they were released from state prisons in fifteen states. This was the largest study of criminal recidivism ever conducted in the United States. The results were alarming: 30 percent of former inmates were rearrested within six months, and 67.5 percent of them were rearrested within three years. Most of the repeat offenders were felons.

Psychologists and criminologists have come to share the belief that most criminals can't change their lives. Although a movement to "rehabilitate" offenders gained momentum in the sixties and seventies, the idea has since largely been abandoned. Now the experts believe that many criminals can't change because they're "psychopaths"—they're unlike the rest of humanity because they aren't burdened by conscience. They don't have any empathy for others. They're concerned only for themselves. In a word, they're *ruthless.*

Psychopaths make up about 1 percent of the overall population, but they're thought to be the norm in prisons. A large number of convicts have been put through "The Hare," the standard test for psychopathy, created by Dr. Robert Hare, a professor at the University of British Columbia, who has been an influential adviser to the Federal Bureau of Investigation. The average score for male inmates in North America is "moderately psychopathic." The experts admit that they really don't know what causes psychopathy. They assume that some people are simply born that way. They also believe that psychopaths can't change to be like the rest of us. This conclusion is powerful and convincing, but if you've lived for a while in San Francisco, you've probably come across a strange exception.

On the waterfront, taking up an entire city block in an enviable location between the Bay Bridge and the Giants' baseball stadium, there's what looks like a luxury condominium complex. The Delancey Street Foundation is actually a residence where criminals live and work together. Most of them have been labeled as "psychopaths." They typically move to Delancey after committing felonies and having serious problems with addiction—to heroin or alcohol, most commonly. Judges send them to Delancey from the state prisons, where they belonged to gangs and perpetrated violence. They're usually the third generation of their families who have known only poverty, crime, and drug addiction. They've never led lawful lives or even understood the values and ideals of lawful society.

They live at Delancey, five hundred of them, blacks and Latinos together with self-proclaimed neo-Nazis, along with only one professional staffer, Dr. Mimi Silbert, who earned PhDs in psychology and criminology before cofounding the program thirty-five years ago. Aside from Silbert, who's sixty-three and stands four feet, eleven and weighs about ninety-five pounds, the felons run the place themselves, without guards or supervisors of any kind.

Delancey Street would sound crazy if it hadn't worked so brilliantly for so long. Silbert entrusts the residents—remember, many of these people have been diagnosed as *psychopaths*—to care for and take responsibility for one another. They kick out anyone who uses drugs, drinks alcohol, or resorts to threats or violence. Although most of them are illiterate when they first arrive, the ex-cons help one another earn their high school equivalency degrees, and they all learn at least three marketable skills. Together they run the top-rated moving company in the Bay Area, a thriving upscale restaurant, a bookstore-café, and a print shop. In the winter they set up sites around the city where they sell Christmas trees. Whenever I'm a customer of a Delancey business, I marvel at the honesty, reliability, and politeness of the workers and wish other companies were like theirs. While taxpayers spend $40,000 a year to support a single prison inmate, Delancey supports itself with profits from its businesses. It never takes money from the government.

After staying at Delancey for four years, most of the residents "graduate" and go out on their own into the greater society. Nearly 60 percent of the people who enter the program make it through and sustain productive lives on the outside.

While the criminal justice system watches more than six out of ten convicts return to crime, Delancey turns nearly as many into lawful citizens. How, exactly? What's the psychology behind transforming the most hopeless 1 percent of society, the ones who experts believe are incapable of change?

·

In the early 1980s the managers at General Motors and the workers on its assembly lines viewed one another with hostility and fear. The situation was especially troubled at the factory in Fremont, California. You could tell this right away by the number of beer bottles littering the parking lot. On any given day, more than a thousand of the five thousand workers wouldn't bother showing up for work. The ones who did show up were distrustful and embittered. They rebelled when their bosses forced them to speed up the production line. They thought GM was trying to eliminate jobs by making the work go faster and by replacing them with robots. They were right: GM's top executives in Detroit blamed the company's problems on its unruly employees, and they were investing a staggering amount of money on automation—$45 billion—so they could cut back on human labor.

Tension pervaded the Fremont plant. Workers and managers battled incessantly. The workers fought with one another so fiercely that the national headquarters of the United Auto Workers had to seize control of the local branch. GM's vice president for labor relations called the plant's workforce "unmanageable." A large percentage of the workers had been there for twenty to twenty-five years, and they were considered impossibly "resistant" to change. Mary-ann Keller, who was Wall Street's most respected analyst of the auto industry, wrote that Fremont was "notorious" even among GM plants. Considering the situation hopeless, GM closed down the factory and laid off five thousand workers.

Then something really strange happened. Toyota offered to revive the plant and produce a GM car there—a Chevrolet. The two companies created a partnership named New United Motor Manufacturing Inc.—"Nummi," which sounded like "new me." Toyota wanted to recruit fresh new hands rather than rehire the plant's laid-off workers. But the UAW insisted otherwise, and Toyota reluctantly took back the ornery old hands.

The workers returned with just as much distrust for their new bosses as they had had for the previous ones. The union leaders believed that the rise of the Japanese car companies had come on the backs of the Japanese workers, whom they thought of as "coolie labor": underpaid and overworked. The workers' fears seemed vindicated when Toyota said it would need only half as many workers as GM to build the same number of cars. When the Toyota people talked about creating a new sense of mutual trust and respect in Fremont, one union leader called it "a load of bullshit."

But that's exactly what happened. Three months after the assembly line started up again, Nummi was rolling out cars with hardly any defects, which was an incredible feat. During this time many GM factories struggled to keep their average down to forty defects a car, and plants would *celebrate* when they had "only" twenty-five defects a car. A *Wall Street Journal* correspondent wrote that Nummi was producing "some of the best cars that GM had ever sold." And Nummi did it with half as many workers. The cost of making the cars fell dramatically. Absenteeism at the Fremont factory went from more than 20 percent down to 2 percent, even though Toyota banned practices that once made the shifts seem tolerable, such as smoking and listening to the radio.

Back at GM's headquarters in Detroit, top executives assumed that Toyota achieved its spectacular results through cutting-edge technology. Detroit sent envoys to Fremont to see what was happening. It turned out that snooping on Japanese technology had been GM's real motive behind making the deal with Toyota in the first place. But there was no gee-whiz gadgetry to see. Nummi's machinery was three decades out of date: It was 1950s technology! The shocking improvements had happened there because the unionized American workers constantly came up with ideas for improving quality and cutting costs. These were the very same workers who had been so hostile and embittered. Now they talked unabashedly about the sense of "family" they felt at the Nummi factory. Toyota's secret wasn't the technology it applied; it was the *psychology*. What did Toyota's executives know that enabled them to win over thousands of workers who had been considered "unmanageable"?

•

The Ornish heart patients, Delancey ex-convicts, and Nummi autoworkers are classic examples of the psychology of change. They may seem like very different situations, but they all show what's gone wrong with our common beliefs on this issue.

We like to think that the facts can convince people to change. We like to think that people are essentially "rational"—that is, they'll act in their self-interest if they have accurate information. We believe that "knowledge is power" and that "the truth will set you free." But nine out of ten heart patients didn't change even when their doctors informed them about what they had to do to prolong their lives. Ex-convicts knew how hard their time could be if they were arrested again, but it didn't make a difference.

After we try "rationally" informing and educating people, we resort to scare tactics. We like to think that change is motivated by fear and that the strongest force for change is crisis, which creates the greatest fear. There are few crises as threatening as heart disease, and no fear as intense as the fear of death, but even those don't motivate heart patients to change.

The fear of losing their jobs didn't compel the Fremont workers to change.

The fear of a long prison sentence didn't intimidate most criminals to "go straight." Even after they were incarcerated for years under awful conditions, they still weren't deterred. What if the laws demanded even harsher punishments? That only made the problem worse, actually. In the decade leading up to the 2002 Justice Department study, the states built more prisons and judges imposed longer sentences. The result? The rearrest rate actually went up by five percentage points, from 62.5 percent to 67.5 percent.

Finally, we often believe that people can't change or that they "resist" change. We think that this is simply human nature. Our most distinguished experts—the MDs and PhDs and MBAs who run the health care and criminal justice systems and the largest manufacturing corporations—think that it's naive and hopeless to expect the vast majority of people to change. They know that patients don't listen to their doctors. In fact, even when patients with severe heart disease are prescribed "statin" drugs, which dramatically lower cholesterol counts and reduce the risk of cardiac arrest, they typically stop following their doctors' orders and give up taking the medication within a year—and all that's involved is popping a little pill once or twice a day.

The people who run things know that ex-cons rebel against the authority of their parole officers. They know that assembly workers struggle against the power of their bosses. So the experts, disgruntled with the ignorance and incorrigibility of the masses, take on the heroic role of saving us from ourselves and from one another. They come up with coronary bypass surgery as a quick fix, or they argue for building more prisons and requiring longer sentences or simply locking up criminals for life, or they try to "automate around the assholes," as one GM executive crudely described the company's grand strategy in the years when it closed down the Fremont plant. They remake their fields around their belief in the impossibility of change. The Ornish and Delancey and Nummi cases are shocking because they prove that dramatic change is possible even in the situations that seem the most hopeless.

•

Change or Die is a short book about a simple idea. Whether it's the average guy who has struggled with a stressful life for so many decades that he has become seriously ill, or the heroin addict who commits felony after felony, or the managers, salespeople, and laborers who try to make it through unnerving shifts in their business, or virtually anyone who comes up against unexpected challenges and opportunities, people can change the deep-rooted patterns of how they think, feel, and act.

I wrote this book because I believe passionately in this idea. My mission is to replace those three misconceptions about change—

our trust in facts, fear, and force (the three Fs)—with what I call "the three keys to change." In the pages that follow I'll introduce you to Mimi Silbert, Dean Ornish, and many others who have come upon the "missing links" of changing behavior. To make sense of these astonishing examples, I'll draw on ideas that have emerged from psychology, cognitive science, linguistics, and neuroscience. I'll show the paradoxical ways in which profound change happens and how we can deliberately influence and inspire change in our own lives, the lives of the people around us, and the lives of our organizations. I'll argue that change can occur with surprising speed and that change can endure.

From the start I want to make it clear that I'm not focusing on how people change on their own. Much of the time, change comes naturally to us. We experiment. We get excited by new ideas and new directions. We learn from experience. We grow and mature. We respond to the new demands of each new stage of our lives, such as college, career, marriage, and parenthood. When we're troubled or distressed and find that our usual solutions aren't working any longer, no matter how hard we try, we seek out new approaches until something works. In *Heartbreak Ridge* Clint Eastwood plays a Marine sergeant who tells his platoon that their motto must be to "adapt, improvise, and overcome," and that's what the rest of us do in real life too. Granted, some people are more adept than others—more resilient, tenacious, or creative—but basically we're all this way. Change often seems to become harder as we get older, but neuroscientists say that there are certain things we can do to sharpen our skillfulness at change as life progresses, and that's what I'll look at later on.

But my main topic is how to change when change *isn't* coming naturally: when the difficulties stubbornly *persist*. When you're *stuck*. When you've tried again and again to overcome problems and all your efforts have failed and the situation appears hopeless or you seem to be powerless. When any reasonable person would think it's an impossible fix. That's what this book is about. I'm going to start by looking in-depth at the three "impossible" cases I've brought up so far—heart patients, drug-addicted criminals, and rebellious autoworkers. As I explain these cases I'll introduce a number of psychological concepts and put more flesh on the bones of a master theory of change. First, though, you need to know the bare bones. This is just a first pass, and these ideas shouldn't make much sense yet. They will become much clearer once we go through the real-world examples. But here, for starters, are the three keys to change, which I call the three Rs: relate, repeat, and reframe.

THE FIRST KEY TO CHANGE
Relate

You form a new, emotional relationship with a person or community that inspires and sustains hope. If you face a situation that a reasonable person would consider "hopeless," you need the influence of seemingly "unreasonable" people to restore your *hope*—to make you *believe* that you can change and *expect* that you will change. This is an act of persuasion—really, it's "selling." The leader or community has to sell you on yourself and make you believe you have the ability to change. They have to sell you on themselves as your partners, mentors, role models, or sources of new knowledge. And they have to sell you on the specific methods or strategies that they employ.

THE SECOND KEY TO CHANGE
Repeat

The new relationship helps you learn, practice, and master the new habits and skills that you'll need. It takes a lot of repetition over time before new patterns of behavior become automatic and seem natural—until you act the new way without even thinking about it. It helps tremendously to have a good teacher, coach, or mentor to give you guidance, encouragement, and direction along the way. Change doesn't involve just "selling"; it requires "training."

THE THIRD KEY TO CHANGE
Reframe

The new relationship helps you learn new ways of thinking about your situation and your life. Ultimately, you look at the world in a way that would have been so foreign to you that it wouldn't have made any sense before you changed.

•

These are the three keys to change: relate, repeat, and reframe. New hope, new skills, and new thinking.

This may sound simple at first, but let me assure you that it's not. Just look at the three examples I've brought up so far: The people who run the health care establishment still don't understand these concepts. Nor do the people who run the criminal justice system. Nor do most of the people who run America's major corporations.

That's all the "theory" you need to get started. Part One, or

"Change 101," will look further at our three cases and build up the theory of change, showing that profound change can happen even in the most difficult situations. Part Two, or "Change 102," will look at how you can change your own life, and how, picking up on recent research in neuroscience, you can improve your knack for change and turn it into an ongoing skill and practice. Then I'll apply the three keys to change to a number of seemingly daunting situations: changing a loved one, changing a company or an organization or a societal institution, and changing an industry or profession. These true stories will take us from the executive offices of companies such as IBM, Yahoo, Amazon.com, and Microsoft to the hallways of charter schools in inner-city neighborhoods and to the desk of a parole officer in Dubuque, Iowa. Through it all we'll see again and again that the same underlying principles of psychology can unlock profound change—and these insights can be grasped easily by anyone.

Unfortunately, no one has been teaching us what we really need to know. People spend billions of dollars every year buying self-help and motivational tapes, videos, and books (such as this one), joining health clubs and diet programs, seeing doctors and therapists, and hiring life coaches and business consultants—and yet so often they fail to realize their goals. The reason isn't that they don't want to change or can't change but rather they don't understand change or have the right tools to effect it.

I was one of those people who repeatedly struggled and failed to change my personal life for many years—even though in my professional life I was expected to know a lot about the subject. When I attended that IBM conference and heard the renowned dean say that very few people can change, it made me wonder for a while about the validity of what I did for a living: I was a staff writer at the monthly business magazine *Fast Company,* which focused on topics of change and innovation. Every month I would write about yet another person who had managed to create profound change within a company or particular business. The stories were supposed to be sources of practical ideas and inspiration for the magazine's hundreds of thousands of subscribers. I would interview iconoclastic entrepreneurs such as Jeff Bezos, the founder of Amazon.com; Richard Branson, the founder of Virgin Atlantic Airways and the Virgin Megastore chain; and Sergey Brin, the cofounder of Google. The reason I had gone to the IBM conference in the first place was that I was in the middle of researching an article about the efforts of IBM's leaders to change the entrenched corporate culture of their 330,000-person organization.

When I heard the experts claim that nine out of ten people can't change, it made me wonder: Can that really be true? If so, the whole point of my work was basically futile. Was I writing every month about people who belonged to that one out of ten for readers who would probably be stuck for the rest of their lives among the other nine out of ten? Were people like Bezos, Branson, and Brin born with some special talent for change that others couldn't emulate no matter what they tried or how hard?

After a few troubled days, it occurred to me that I belonged to that one out of ten. Actually, I have earned a place in an even more selective cohort: I am part of the 3 percent of Americans who have lost weight (in my case, forty pounds) and kept it off for at least five years (the figures come from the National Institutes for Health). Three percent calculates to roughly one out of thirty-three. Although I don't really believe in astrology, I was the classic Taurus—

exceptionally stubborn and gluttonous—and I thought: If I can change, then surely anyone can change. Maybe they just needed the inspiration of a terrific teacher and role model like the personal trainer I finally hired after a decade of failed struggles against obesity.

Then I tried to think of case studies that contradicted what the Johns Hopkins dean was saying. I was familiar with Dean Ornish's ideas because I lived just down the street from the University of California at San Francisco's medical school, and a number of my friends were doctors or students there. I also knew about Delancey Street because I had hired its ex-convicts as movers and had eaten at their restaurant and bought several Christmas trees from them. When I researched the figures about the success rates of those two programs, the odds for change totally flipped—assuming you knew what Dean Ornish and Mimi Silbert knew. The great need for spreading that knowledge much more widely through the populace inspired the research for this book.

Change or Die began as a cover story for *Fast Company* debunking what I called our most common "myths" about how to motivate change, especially our reliance on facts and fear. I had strong notions about what failed to promote profound change, but I still needed a guide to what really worked and why. Ultimately, the best one I found was a book, first published in 1961, called *Persuasion & Healing* by Jerome D. Frank, MD, who had been a professor of psychiatry at Johns Hopkins University.

That's right: Hopkins. It's sadly ironic that I could attend a prestigious conference in 2004 and hear the dean of the medical school and chief of the hospital at Hopkins bemoan that we still don't understand how to inspire people to change. The truth is that psychologists know *exactly* how to do it, and they've known how for a long time. The breakthrough insights sprang from research conducted half a century ago by Dr. Frank at that very institution. Frank was still alive and in his nineties when the new dean publicly revealed an ignorance of his brilliant work.

Jerome Frank ran the psychiatric outpatient clinic at the university's hospital in the 1950s. His fascinating research began with a fairly simple, small study. His team wanted to learn what really worked in psychological therapy (which literally means "mind-changing" and is better known simply as "psychotherapy"). So they decided to compare "three forms of therapy as different as we could make them," he wrote. The first method was the classic approach, made famous by Sigmund Freud himself, where the patient meets with the therapist in intensive private sessions. The second method was group therapy, a newer strategy that was just starting to attract interest at the time. It gathered a bunch of patients together for long conversations moderated by a professional. The third method was an even more experimental idea of "minimal" therapy with the patient meeting with a doctor for sessions that were unusually short (only half an hour) and infrequent (once every two weeks).

The researchers asked the patients to fill out ratings about how much the therapy had helped them overcome their symptoms, such as anxiety and distress. The therapists scored their patients' progress as well, as did independent third-party experts (social workers, who also interviewed the patients). When the numbers were added up, Frank and his Hopkins colleagues felt "astonishment and chagrin," he recalled, because the results weren't anything like what they had expected to find. It turned out that all three kinds of therapy worked just as well even though they were so different from one another. The researchers had been looking for a clear winner, but all three had won.

Frank's initial study was small and relatively crude. But in the following decades the psychology profession put an impressive amount of energy, money, time, and brainpower into studying the effectiveness of the more than four hundred different schools of psychotherapy, and the results were still the same: Every kind of psychotherapy was helpful to patients, but no particular kind was significantly more helpful than others. By the 1970s psychologists had begun calling this finding the "Do-Do Verdict," after the scene in *Alice's Adventures in Wonderland* where the Do-Do bird declares, "Everybody has won and all must have prizes."

But Jerome Frank had already correctly guessed this finding soon after his own initial study way back in the 1950s. Frank had the notion that the whole point of his study was wrong: What if various kinds of therapy worked because of what they had in common with one another, not what made them different? What if it was deceptive that they looked so different because they actually shared the same "active ingredients" that made them effective? If so, then what was the secret sauce in these different recipes?

The common denominator, it turned out, was that going to therapy inspired a new sense of hope for the patients—the belief and expectation that they would overcome their troubles. The key factor was the chemistry of the emotionally charged relationship formed by the patient and the therapist or the group, not the specific theories or techniques that differentiated the particular school of therapy.

Frank was interested in anthropology, and he applied these ideas not only to Western medicine and psychiatry but also to religious and shamanic healing, which he identified as psychotherapies from different cultures. The same principles also applied brilliantly in those traditions. A preacher and a congregation, a shaman and the assembled tribesmen of an Amazon village, or a therapist and a group therapy meeting could equally inspire a distressed person.

Frank's breakthrough ideas have spawned a prodigious amount of fascinating scientific research about the importance of inspiring hope and belief, the "common factors," and the therapeutic relationship. Some of this work was collected in the thick 1999 anthology *The Heart & Soul of Change: What Works in Therapy,* published by the American Psychological Association.

So we know what works in therapy. I wanted to look further and also see what works *outside* of therapy. Couldn't a troubled person be inspired to change by having a positive relationship with someone other than a psychologist? Having spent nearly two decades as a journalist covering the business world, I wanted to see whether, and how, these ideas could apply to bringing about change in companies and organizations. The best research on this topic had been led by John Kotter, a professor at Harvard Business School, who concluded that changing organizations depends overwhelmingly on changing the emotions of their individual members. This alerted me to the plausibility of a unified theory of how both individuals and groups of people can change, something that the Harvard cognitive scientist Howard Gardner had already worked toward in his research.

In coming up with the "three keys to change," I began with Frank's principles of effective psychotherapy and stripped away the elements that apply only to more formal kinds of therapy, such as the usefulness of "a healing setting"—a special place where the patient feels safe and protected (such as a doctor's office). Then I tried to reduce the essentials of his theory into a more streamlined formulation, and I tested it out against the wide range of real-world case studies I've researched for this book. When I interviewed people like Ornish and Silbert, their explanations fit the theory well. Within this framework I've also tried to incorporate important ideas from the fields of cognitive science, neuroscience, and linguistics, which have emerged in the time since Frank's initial study and are providing new and extremely useful tools in psychology.

The result, I hope, is a master theory of change that readers can easily understand and apply in their own lives.

PART ONE

Change 101

IF THEY CAN CHANGE, SO CAN YOU

Case Studies: Heart Patients, Criminals, and Workers

CASE STUDY:

Heart Patients

Richard began smoking when he was a teenager. When he was in his twenties and thirties, he smoked as much as three packs a day. After he suffered a heart attack at the age of thirty-seven, he finally quit the habit—well, at least for a while. He had a second heart attack at forty-three. Following his third heart attack, at forty-seven, he underwent quadruple coronary artery bypass surgery.

Following the operation Richard resumed a lifestyle that worsened his heart condition. He didn't get much exercise. He gained forty pounds. He continued working as a powerful executive, which subjected him to heavy stress and frequent crises. But he was a very lucky man, and his grafts lasted for a dozen years, which was longer than his doctors might have expected. Then, at fifty-nine, Richard was struck by his fourth heart attack. He was rushed to the hospital at four thirty in the morning, and he underwent another operation—this time the surgeons inserted a steel stent to make way for blood to flow through. But the artery clogged up again within three months. Richard felt sharp chest pains, each lasting as long as five minutes. It turned out that the artery was 90 percent blocked. He was taken to the hospital for another medical emergency—"unstable angina"—and surgeons had to redo the procedure. Three months later, his doctors found that he had an irregular heartbeat that could kill him, so they implanted a defibrillator under the skin of his chest—a small electronic device that shocks his heart back to a steady rhythm.

Finally, Richard pursued a healthier lifestyle. It helped that he was a top executive and his organization provided personal chefs who prepared salads for him, doctors who followed him wherever he went, and assistants who hauled his heavy, hulking exercise machine—an "elliptical cross trainer"—onto his private airplane to make sure he could get in his thirty-minute daily workout even when he was traveling around the world, which he often had to do. He was independently wealthy, and he could easily afford to retire to a life of hunting and fishing on his ranch and maybe serving on a few corporate boards. Instead he held onto his job, which had become increasingly stressful. He often responded to the pressure by venting his anger, such as the embarrassing time when he cursed out one of his colleagues in public. When Richard was sixty-three, one of the nation's top cardiologists reviewed his history and said, "It's a testament to medical science that he's alive."

As you may have guessed, Richard's last name is Cheney, he prefers to be called "Dick," and he's worked as the White House chief of staff, secretary of defense, and vice president of the United States.

This chapter is about heart patients and what does—and

doesn't—motivate them to change how they live. There are two reasons why I've singled out Cheney from among the sixty-two million Americans who suffer from heart disease. First, I want to talk about how our minds work—how we think about our lives and our world—and politics is a familiar way of introducing a notion that I want to apply to many other topics. That notion is ideology.

Psych Concept #1

Frames

As soon as you hear "Dick Cheney"—the name of a controversial political figure in a time of crisis and combat—you probably have a strong gut-level emotional reaction one way or the other. It reflects your "ideology"—the complicated web of entrenched ideas that conditions how you think and feel.

We're guided by ideologies about all kinds of matters, not just politics, and they're vital to understanding change. Instead of "ideology" you can refer to it as a "belief system" or a "conceptual framework" ("frames," for short). Whatever you call them, these are the "mental structures that shape how we view the world" in the words of Berkeley professor George Lakoff. A psychologist would say that our deep-rooted beliefs are part of "the cognitive unconscious." A neuroscientist would say "the long-term concepts that structure how we think are instantiated in the synapses of the brain." A plainer speaker would say that our true beliefs are what we feel deep in our guts, and they're hard to change because they've developed over a lifetime.

That helps to explain why simply providing information doesn't sway how people think and feel. You can give the same facts to liberals and conservatives but people on each side will interpret the facts to support their own beliefs. Look at the varying responses to *March of the Penguins,* a documentary that shows how father and mother penguins each take turns waddling back and forth across 70 miles of ice to find food while the partner stays home protecting the fertilized egg in 70-degree-below-zero temperatures. Political conservatives loved the film and helped make it a surprise blockbuster. Michael Medved, a conservative radio talk show host, praised the movie because it "passionately affirms traditional norms like monogamy, sacrifice, and child rearing." Rich Lowry, editor of the right-wing *National Review,* told an audience of young conservatives, "It's an amazing movie. And I have to say, penguins are really the ideal example of monogamy." Other conservatives lauded the film as an emotional case against abortion.

What's interesting is that liberals saw the same movie and thought it was *liberal* propaganda. When the male and female penguins take turns going out into the greater world and staying home with their progeny—wasn't that an affirmation of progressive ideas about gender roles? Even though the penguins sacrificed to bring new lives into being, they all mated with different partners every year, which suggested a more permissive "serial monogamy" that liberals said clashed with conservative morality.

We take the facts and fit them into the frames we already have. If the facts don't fit, we're likely to challenge whether they're really facts or to dismiss the information and persist somehow in believing what we want to believe. I found this when none of my friends could remember that my wife, Susan, and I were spending two years living in Roanoke, Virginia—a small city in a remote part of the Appalachian mountains. I told everyone that we were moving there so Susan could study for her master's degree at Hollins University, a small women's college that had a very reputable graduate program in her field of creative writing. My friends, whom I had first met when we were in college together or during the fifteen years I lived in San Francisco and Manhattan, had never heard of Roanoke or Hollins. During those two years they frequently called and asked how we liked living in Charlottesville (which is one hundred miles away from Roanoke) and how Susan liked it there at the University of Virginia. They didn't believe that "people like us" went to graduate school in Virginia unless it was at the University of Virginia, which they knew about because of its top-ranked programs in business, medicine, and law. They had a particular vision of how the world worked, and it told them that people who had gone to Ivy League colleges and lived in major global cities only moved to provincial towns to enroll at top law, medical, or business schools. No matter how many times I repeated "Roanoke" and "Hollins," their brains transformed the data into "Charlottes-ville" and "University of Virginia."

"Concepts are not things that can be changed just by someone telling us a fact," says Lakoff, who's a pro-fessor of cognitive science and linguistics. "We may be presented with facts, but for us to make sense of them, they have to fit what is already in the synapses of the brain. Otherwise, facts go in and then they go right back out. They are not heard, or they are not accepted as facts, or they mystify us: Why would anyone have said that? Then we label the fact as irrational, crazy, or stupid."

The other reason I began this chapter with Dick Cheney's medical history was to show that when it comes to how we think and feel about health, the vast majority of us share the same belief system as he does. In politics we might be liberals or conservatives, Democrats or Republicans, left-wingers or right-wingers, with shadings and subtleties, of course. But nearly all of us have a deep conviction about the awesome power of science and technology, and that includes a strong belief in "scientific medicine."

From the breakthroughs of earlier eras (antibiotics, X-rays, open-heart surgery) to the marvels of recent years (antidepressants, DNA testing, fMRI brain scans), scientific medicine has repeat-edly startled us with its capabilities. Some of your earliest child-hood memories probably involve your parents taking you to doctors, who made you feel better, and those experiences influ-enced your lasting gut-level emotions and beliefs. Every society in recorded history has had a class of healers, who've often relied on magic, faith, or plants. In the scientific age, our healers have been physicians, and they've relied on expensive technology and pharmaceuticals.

Scientific medicine so nearly monopolized the health business that it became known in the United States and other Western nations simply as "Western" medicine. Only in recent years, with the rise of "alternative" medicine, have many people even realized that there are other ways to think about healing. Still, most of us feel suspicious about or even outright condemn people who shun Western medicine, such as Christian Scientists, and think they're negligent for refusing to take their children to doctors.

Throughout our lives we've had extraordinary admiration and respect for physicians and made them into an elite class in our societies. For the past twenty-two years an independent firm called MORI has conducted a poll in Britain, and every year the poll has found that medicine is the most trusted profession. In the 2005 survey of more than two thousand people ages fifteen and older, 91 percent said they trusted doctors to tell the truth, which put physicians ahead of everyone else:

Physicians	91%
Teachers	88%
Professors	77%
Judges	76%
Priests and other clergy	73%
Scientists	70%
Television news anchors	63%
The police	58%
The ordinary person in the street	56%

Pollsters	50%
Civil servants	44%
Trade union officials	37%
Business leaders	24%
Politicians and government ministers	20%
Journalists	16%

When the Harris Poll company conducted a similar survey among Americans, who are markedly less trustful than the British, 77 percent said they trusted doctors to tell the truth, ranking doctors second only to teachers at 80 percent. When Harris focused on Americans who are fifty-five and older—the group that relies the most on doctors—it found that 93 percent of them trust their physicians.

Given this background, let's take another look at the case of patients with severe heart disease. Let's say, for the sake of illustration, that you're one of them. For many years, decades even, you tried repeatedly to live healthier but your efforts have failed, and now you're suffering from awful pain. In the lingo of psychologists, you're "demoralized," meaning that you're overwhelmed by feelings of hopelessness and powerlessness. You need to seek out other people who can inspire new hope. People with the power to relieve your pain and heal you: *doctors.*

From the very start, every aspect of the healing process reinforces the belief that you're powerless and the doctors are all-powerful. It casts you as helpless, and the doctors as heroic. You're entirely passive, while doctors are active.

You start as a supplicant. You make a pilgrimage to a sacred healing place, a complex of massive buildings connected to a prestigious university, a center of knowledge. You wait to meet with the elite class of healers, who are set apart by their special attire. Their offices are lined with framed diplomas attesting to the exceptional skills they developed through many years of arduous education, testing, and apprenticeship. While you believe there's nothing you can do to help yourself, the doctors inspire your belief and expectation that they will heal you. The surgeries they perform are amazing. Implanting a piece of plastic to prop open your artery—that's *astonishing*. Removing a vein from your leg and stitching it near your heart so the blood can bypass the blocked passage—that's *stunning*. After the operation you no longer feel the terrible pain and you can climb stairs again and play tennis. Miraculous! Then they prescribe a "statin" pill that can reduce your cholesterol and lower your risk of having a heart attack. Magical! Even though you're accustomed to the spectacular achievements of science and technology, you're awestruck by these demonstrations of power.

After performing the miracle surgeries and prescribing the miracle drugs, the doctors remind you: By the way, now you've got to start living in a healthier way. Even though the doctors are doing their duty by mouthing these words, they don't really believe that you can change. They know about the studies saying there's a 90 percent probability you won't change. They've seen this firsthand in the hundreds or thousands of patients they've treated over the course of their careers. It's very difficult to inspire a belief in others that you don't believe yourself. Their lack of conviction, betrayed by the look in their eyes or the tone of their voices or their body language, takes away from the impact of their words. Besides, what's more persuasive: their words or their actions? The surgery and the drugs convey the message that you really don't have to change. They were invented because you can't or won't change. (And you know it's true. In your gut you believe that you can't change your lifestyle.) The insurance company paid so much for the operations, and will pay for expensive medications that you'll need to take for the rest of your life, because you can't change. Besides, if you had the power to heal yourself, then why did you go through the trauma of having your chest sliced open and sewn back together again?

Doctors know that they're not magical healers. They can relieve symptoms—chest pain in the case of heart patient—but they usually don't "cure" people of disease. However, our mythology about medicine (our belief system) casts doctors as potent healers and we expect them to heal us. We believe they'll cure us. After the doctors have taken their heroic efforts with heart surgery, then you're no longer in pain, so you *feel* as if you're cured.

The doctors are trained to perform surgery or prescribe drugs. That's what they learn in medical school and during their residencies at hospitals. That's what they excel at. That's what they believe in. They aren't trained in psychology. So it's not surprising that they make two of the most common mistakes when they try to motivate people to change their behavior. They rely on facts and fear—in the case of their heart patients, doctors rely on fear of death. Fear works, but only for a brief time. For a few weeks following a heart attack or heart surgery, patients are so scared that they will do whatever their doctors tell them. But death is too frightening to think about for very long, so they avoid thinking about it. They go into "denial" and revert to their unhealthy behavior, which comes easy since the *pain is gone!* Hallelujah! They feel healed!

Psych Concept #2

Denial and Other Psychological Self-defenses

When we find ourselves in seemingly intolerable situations and feel overwhelmed by tension, anxiety, and a sense of powerlessness, or when the harsh realities of our lives threaten to crush our self-esteem, our minds unconsciously activate a number of powerful, built-in, automatic psychological strategies to help us cope. We shield ourselves from the threatening and humiliating facts. We banish the bad news from our conscious awareness. For example, heart patients avoid thinking about how their disease threatens to kill them. Of course, the threat doesn't have to be that extreme. After I go to the dentist for a checkup and he warns me about my receding gum line, I worry about it enough to floss my teeth for the next two or three nights. But then the fear and the flossing end.

Freud called these coping mechanisms "ego defenses," and even though so many of his ideas have been discredited throughout the past century, this one particular idea has survived all the critics and become accepted as hard fact. Freud's daughter, Anna, wrote a book in 1936 that cataloged the "defenses." Since then psychologists keep discovering more of these ingenious strategies. On the bookshelf above my desk I keep a heavy 572-page tome, first published in 1970, entitled *The Ego and Its Defenses,* that analyzes forty-eight different defenses. Some of the categories are familiar to everyone.

We all know about number three, "denial"—literally, denying that a problem exists. The term has become part of the popular vocabulary and pops up in movies and television shows. We all know about number seven, "idealization," which happens when you've fallen so madly in love with the wrong person that you're blind to the person's faults and misdeeds even though they're blatantly clear to your friends and family. And who among us hasn't been guilty, now or then, of number thirteen, "projection"—blaming other people for our own faults? And does a day go by before every one of us engages in number fourteen, "rationalization," or coming up with creative excuses to cover up the real motives for our behavior? (Psychologists often joke that humans aren't "rational beings." We're "rationalizing beings.")

I like paging through *The Ego and Its Defenses* so I can amuse myself by trying to figure out how many of the strategies I've deployed at earlier times in my own life. But the book doesn't help with what's happening *today*. Even though we've all heard about "denial," and many of us like to bandy about the term in casual conversation, what most people don't grasp is that denial and other psychological self-defenses aren't intentional choices. We're not consciously aware that we're deploying mental mechanisms to relieve us from overwhelming anxiety. Ego defenses are how our unconscious minds alleviate the debilitating burdens of our conscious minds. Our brains automatically push certain unappealing knowledge out of our waking thoughts and we don't even realize it.

Remember the famous scene in the movie *A Few Good Men* when Tom Cruise asks Jack Nicholson to tell him the truth and Nicholson replies, "You can't handle the truth"? That's what the unconscious mind is saying. When the conscious mind can't handle the truth, it's spared the truth. The unconscious comes to the emotional rescue.

Now you can study the 572 pages of *The Ego and Its Defenses* for countless hours, and you can even get a PhD in psychology from a prestigious university, but knowing how the mind works isn't going to change how *your* mind works. Even the most learned experts unwittingly protect their egos through denial, idealization, projection, rationalization, and all the other self-defense strategies, just as the rest of us do. Consider the case of Kay Redfield Jamison, who is luminously intelligent and has a PhD in psychology from the University of California at Los Angeles. While she was a professor in the hospital's psychiatric clinic, she refused to believe that she suffered from manic depression, an illness she was trained to diagnose. Even though she faced a "change or die" situation—the depressive episodes made her suicidal—she spent years refusing to take lithium, the medication prescribed to her by her doctors. In her extraordinary memoir *An Unquiet Mind,* she writes about her "fundamental denial that what I had was a real disease."

When you have a potentially fatal illness, denial can be deadly; but under more normal circumstances, denial is actually a good thing for us (at least to a certain degree). Without denial, it would be much more difficult for any intelligent, well-informed person to achieve the peace of mind necessary to get through the day. We all live in denial about many scary things. For the past several years, Americans have been well aware of the potential for terrorist attacks on home soil. For the past several decades, we've lived with the danger of intentional or accidental launching of nuclear weapons. There's always the possibility that one day we could find ourselves amid a terrorist slaughter or a nuclear holocaust, and there's probably not much any of us, whether ordinary citizens or political leaders, can do about it. Everyone has worried about these dangers at some point, but few of us think about it on a daily basis. We put threats of suicide bombers and atomic attacks out of our minds so we can get out of bed in the mornings and get on with the challenges and pleasures of our daily lives.

If we constantly worried about everything that's constantly threatening us—nuclear proliferation, terrorism, global warming, and the conflicts and crises described in most of the articles in the first section of the *New York Times*—then we'd have trouble calming down and summoning the focus, energy, and positive outlook to cook breakfast or drive to the office. Basic psychological health *demands* a certain level of denial. It's likewise helpful, up to a certain point, when we deceive ourselves about our own flaws, since that makes it easier for us to maintain a necessary self-confidence and optimism.

But while our defense mechanisms are helpful in the short run—getting us through the day or the week—

they block us from solving our persistent problems. Denial is one of the biggest reasons it's so difficult to motivate other people to change. We think we can enlighten them by telling them the facts, but they're in denial because they've already confronted the facts and *they can't handle the facts.* We try to use fear to motivate them to change, but they're in denial because *the fear is too overwhelming.*

When a person is demoralized and feels a sense of hopelessness and powerlessness about a seemingly impossible situation, then the common responses are depression and defeatism or denial and defense. The way to overcome either of these fates isn't through hearing the facts or being aroused by fear. If you're hopeless, then what you need is someone to inspire a new sense of hope—the belief and expectation that you can change your situation and overcome the difficulties you've struggled with. And that's exactly what happens in the first key to change.

Even when you've studied psychological self-defense, it's still an eye-opener to see how widespread and dangerous these mechanisms are—especially in the case of patients who have severe heart disease. What's really astonishing is that they don't even take the drugs (called "statins") their doctors prescribe for them, which have a good chance of saving their lives. A study of 37,000 patients who were prescribed five different popular "brands" of statins (Lipitor, Lescol, Mevacor, Pravachol, and Zocor) in October 1997 found that nearly everyone took the pills for the first month or two, but by

December, around half of them had stopped. By October 1998, one full year later, only one fifth to one third of the patients were still taking their prescribed medication, which they were supposed to keep taking *for the rest of their lives.*

What could possibly be a smaller or an easier lifestyle change than popping a pill every day? Americans spend more than $200 billion a year on prescription drugs. Don't we love our pills? Only when they make us feel better. Statins don't make you feel any different, except for their side effects, which are usually mild. But taking pills reminds you that you have a chronic illness, a deadly disease, and you don't want to be reminded.

As armchair observers it's easy to feel superior to the seeming "irrationality" of other people. The reality is that even the smartest of us—the ones with the best educations, the sharpest, quickest minds, and the greatest abilities for digesting and analyzing loads of complex information—are likely to act this way. Walt Mossberg fits this description. Mossberg was a star reporter at the *Wall Street Journal,* where he proved his versatility by covering beats that included the auto industry, labor, defense, and economics. There seemed to be no subject matter that he couldn't master quickly. He gained renown by writing "Personal Technology," a column that demystified computers. When he began reviewing high-tech products for the average consumer, his expert opinions made him one of the most powerful figures in Silicon Valley. He gained so many loyal readers, who in turn attracted so many lucrative advertisers, that he was considered vital to the *Journal's* fortunes. To compete with a rival offer, the newspaper made Mossberg its highest-paid staffer with a salary reported to be more than $500,000, more than the pay of his boss, Paul Steiger, the managing editor.

In 2004 *Wired* magazine assigned me to write a profile of Mossberg. He was cooperative and smoothed the way for me to interview his wife, his editor, his friends, and his current and former colleagues at the newspaper. But Mossberg hadn't anticipated one thing that the people close to him would reveal: They were worried about his poor health habits. In 1997, at the age of fifty, he had suffered a major heart attack. His doctors performed quadruple coronary bypass surgery, transplanting a vein from one of his arms. When Mossberg returned to work three months later, Steiger observed that "his spirits were very strong and his health seemed much stronger."

For a while Mossberg dieted and slimmed down to what one of his colleagues referred to as "the sleek new Walt." But before long he was overweight and sedentary again. When I asked his wife, Edie, how much the heart attack had changed him, she said, "It should have changed him more. When you first come out of it, you're healthy, healthy! Now he slides back and forth." Mossberg himself admitted, "I'm bad at diet and exercise."

He didn't switch to a less stressful lifestyle. He remained intensely driven. He wrote all his columns on tight deadlines the day before they had to be published. He had no backlog stored up to take off the constant pressure. He typically began work at 7:00 A.M., and he often worked from home at night and sent e-mails until 1:00 A.M. After the heart attack and bypass surgery, he *increased* his workload. He added a third weekly column and began organizing and hosting an annual conference for Silicon Valley executives.

Mossberg was very amiable with me, sitting for a marathon interview in person and responding at length by e-mail to follow-up questions. But when he found out I was asking around about his health habits, he turned angry and combative. He questioned why his health was relevant, even though it was obviously a valid concern for executives and shareholders of his company, since their profits depended greatly on it. He explained that the men in his family had a history of heart problems that struck them when they were still young; his brother, for example, was slender and fit but still had suffered a heart attack. I argued that while your genes may put you at greater risk for having heart problems, it doesn't mean you can't reduce those risks by the way you live. If you had bad luck with your genes, why not try even harder to live healthier? But facts and fear hadn't led Mossberg to change, and neither would "force"—the verbal pressure exerted on him by friends, family, and colleagues. Even though he was a famed critic, he shrank from self-criticism when it mattered. And even though he had a very rational mind, he was nonetheless in denial.

·

So far we've seen that conventional doctors fail to motivate nine out of ten heart patients to change their lifestyles. The doctors rely on facts and fear, but those tactics don't work because patients resort to the psychological self-defense of denial. The whole conceptual framework of Western medicine further hampers doctors' efforts because it casts doctors in active, heroic roles and relegates patients to passive, hopeless roles. Trained thoroughly in this mindset, which is second nature to them, doctors don't believe patients can change, which in turn doesn't help patients believe they can.

Now we're ready to meet Dr. Ornish.

Dean Ornish's story is all about change on every level: how he changed his own life, how he's helped heart patients change their lives, and how he's been trying for three decades to change the health care system in the United States.

I always feel uneasy about meeting the public figures I've long admired because I'm afraid of discovering they don't live up to the ideals that they espouse for the rest of us. So I was nervous when Dean Ornish's assistant told me that he was too busy to meet in person for the interview we had scheduled weeks ahead. Ornish was working from his home in Sausalito, California, across the Golden Gate Bridge from San Francisco, and apparently he was so pressed for time that he couldn't take a few minutes to travel the few blocks to his office in that same little town. Instead we would conduct the interview over the phone. Ornish began by asking whether I was planning to tape record the conversation. *No,* I said. I can quickly scribble my own amateur shorthand. Ornish volunteered to make a tape for me, warning that he was going to talk very quickly. He was right: The man is one of the fastest talkers I've ever encountered. A stenographer would probably sweat while trying to transcribe his outpouring of words. I wondered: What would he have been like if he didn't relieve stress through yoga and meditation? Surely he would have had a heart attack.

The way Ornish describes it, he would have been dead.

Raised in an affluent family in Dallas—his father was a dentist, and his mother was a writer and historian—Ornish aspired to become a doctor. But the intense pressure of his "pre-med" studies made him sleepless and nearly psychotic. He felt unhappy, depressed, helpless, hopeless, powerless, anxious, fearful, worried, and lonely. He dropped out of college, moved back home, and contemplated committing suicide. Then he met his older sister's yoga instructor, Swami Satchidananda. The spiritual teacher seemed "serene, radiant, and peaceful," Ornish thought. "A very loving and wise soul."

What happened next was a classic example of the three keys to change.

KEY #1
Relate

Ornish became a follower of the swami, who inspired in him a new sense of hope—the belief and expectation that he could change.

KEY #2
Repeat

The swami helped him learn and practice vegetarianism, yoga, and meditation. These new habits and skills made him feel healthier and more relaxed and psychologically balanced on a daily basis. Ornish gave up his meaty "Texas diet of chili, cheeseburgers, and chalupas."

KEY #3
Reframe

The swami helped him learn about Eastern philosophy, a new way of thinking about his situation and his life. This gave Ornish a sense of purpose and perspective and relieved his depression.

With his morale restored Ornish returned to college. He graduated summa cum laude from the University of Texas at Austin and entered medical school at Baylor. He was lucky enough to be assigned for a clinical "rotation" working in the hospital with Dr. Michael DeBakey, one of the most famous heart surgeons of all time. In the 1960s DeBakey had performed the first aortic coronary artery bypass and appeared on the cover of *Time*. In 1977, with the twenty-four-year-old Dean Ornish assisting, DeBakey performed many more. "We would cut people open and bypass their blocked arteries," Ornish recalled. "Then they would go home, eat the same food, not manage stress, not exercise, and smoke. More often than not, their bypasses would re-occlude"—clog up again—"and we would redo them, sometimes multiple times."

At the end of his second year of medical school, Ornish took time off to conduct a study and see whether what he had learned from the swami could help heart patients. He recruited ten people whose heart disease was so bad that surgeons wouldn't operate on them. Their disease had spread so widely that they didn't have any good veins left to graft. They suffered attacks of "angina"—bouts of terrible, prolonged chest pains—seven to ten times a day.

Ornish moved them into a block of rooms at the Plaza Hotel in Houston and lived with them there, day and night, for a full month. He brought in a chef to prepare low-fat vegetarian cuisine for all their meals. Every morning and afternoon he led them in yoga and exercise classes and gave lectures on the scientific rationale for what they were doing.

Every evening the patients sat in a circle for a group discussion.

Ornish had intended these meetings as a chance for people to exchange recipes and diet tips and compare notes about running shoes. But soon the patients began confiding in one another about their emotions: depression, loneliness, unhappiness, anxiety, and fear. Exactly what Ornish himself had suffered from a few years earlier. Unwittingly he had created a psychological "support group."

Not everyone liked the austere diet served by Ornish's chef. Late at night a few of the participants would sneak down to the hotel's bar for pepperoni pizza and booze. Still, when the thirty days were over, the results were astonishing: a 91 percent decrease in the frequency of the awful chest pains.

Ornish's professors told him not to try to publish his study since it had too few patients and because the results were too incredible to be believed.

In 1980, when he graduated from medical school, Ornish concocted a bigger and better study. This time he took twenty-three patients to a hotel in the Texas "hill country"—an isolated rural setting where they couldn't sneak off and eat pizza. From there, Ornish could control what they ate: a vegan diet (no animal products) with the one exception of nonfat yogurt. They spent five hours a day learning and practicing "stress management techniques": yoga, meditation, and visualization. The study lasted only twenty-four days, but the results were spectacular. The frequency of chest pains fell by 91 percent *again*, the same result as the previous study. Cholesterol levels fell 25 percent. Blood pressure decreased. The patients were able to exercise 44 percent longer than they could when the study began.

Ornish's work attracted the interest of some important people, such as Dr. Alexander Leaf, the chairman of medicine at the Harvard Medical School and the Massachusetts General Hospital, who flew to Texas to see firsthand what Ornish was up to. Later he became Ornish's mentor. Still, most of the medical establishment remained highly skeptical. It was one thing to lock up a bunch of patients in a remote setting and starve them for a month, but surely Ornish couldn't get anyone to stick to his regime while going on with their lives in the real world for longer stretches of time.

In 1986 Ornish began a new trial in San Francisco, where he had become a professor at the University of California medical school. This time he took heart patients to a hotel for a weeklong orientation. Afterward the patients went back to their own homes. They got together twice a week for support groups with a psychologist. Ornish asked them to practice yoga or meditation for an hour a day and to exercise at least three hours a week. He insisted on a nearly vegan diet. And they had to live that way for a year.

One of the participants was a man named Werner Hebenstreit. He had suffered from chest pains for an entire decade. He had suffered his first heart attack five years earlier, at the age of sixty-eight, and his second one that year at seventy-two. "The heart attacks did me in psychologically," he later recalled. "I was filled with anger and self-pity. And I was enraged at the medical profession, which didn't help me." When his wife said that a Dr. Ornish was on the phone, Hebenstreit refused to take the call. "My wife said he was our doctor's friend, and that I should at least find out why he was calling. I got on the phone and said, 'Dr. Ornish, whatever you are selling, I am not buying.'" But Ornish, passionate and persuasive, talked him into taking part in the trial.

"The support groups were especially hard for me," Hebenstreit said. "I had been a typical loner and kept a tight lid on my emotions." He was angry about his illness. As a Jewish native of Germany, he felt guilty for surviving the Holocaust while millions perished. Four decades after the end of World War II, he still felt rage at the Nazis.

The Ornish program exorcised the demons and inspired a new sense of hope for Hebenstreit. His cholesterol count fell from 320 to 145 and stayed there. (Anything below 200 is considered within safe range.)

The study's results were published in a major scientific journal, the *Lancet,* and they were impressive: The patients who took part in the one-year experiment had a 91 percent decrease in frequency of chest pains. The magic number, 91 percent, kept coming up again and again. And 82 percent of the patients had arteries that weren't as clogged as they were when the study began.

Could the patients stick with the difficult program? And how! Even though they were left to prepare their own meals, the percentage of fat in their diet fell from 30 to 6 percent, their daily consumption of cholesterol fell from 211 to 3 milligrams, and they lost an average of twenty-four pounds.

The weekly meetings lasted only a year, but Ornish kept tracking the patients for five years and proved that they had changed their lifestyles for good. After five years 99 percent had stopped or reversed the progress of their heart disease. They practiced yoga or meditation five times a week for forty-nine minutes a day. Their intake of cholesterol remained at fewer than 10 percent of what it had been. They kept off about thirteen of the twenty-four pounds they had lost, which is a rare achievement. (A National Institutes of

Health study showed that 97 percent of people who lose weight wind up gaining it all back within five years.)

Werner Hebenstreit's improvements were terrific. After five years, the blockage of his arteries had fallen from 54 to 13 percent. After fifteen years, at age eighty-six, he still got together with the alumni of his support group. His daily routine was vigorous: He would wake up at 6:00 A.M. to do push-ups, yoga, and meditation before breakfast. He and his wife walked together for half an hour every day, and once a week he went out on a hike for more than four hours.

Ornish's studies had profound effects on their participants but little impact on the health industry. His critics argued that the hippies in San Francisco might be willing to eat tofu and do yoga but it wouldn't work in the heartland. The insurers refused to pay for his program even though they paid for heart surgery and drugs. But then Dr. Kenneth McDonough, the medical director of the Mutual of Omaha insurance company, became interested in Ornish's ideas and went to a retreat that Ornish ran in California. McDonough even tried the Ornish diet himself. In less than a year he lost twenty-five pounds, going from 180 to 155. At his direction Mutual of Omaha agreed to pay for another trial, this time testing Ornish's ideas at eight sites that covered the full diversity of America, including Omaha, Des Moines, and Columbia, South Carolina, where one cardiologist warned, "Gravy is a beverage here, so this will be a big change in their diet."

Ornish's team studied 333 patients whose insurance programs were willing to pay for them to have coronary bypasses or angioplasties: 194 volunteered to try Ornish's regime while the other 139 underwent heart surgery. The average age of the volunteers was only fifty-eight years, but their medical records were frightening and intimidating:

50% suffered from hypertension
20% had diabetes
66% had smoked cigarettes
58% had family histories of heart disease
55% had already suffered heart attacks

Ornish trained teams in each location that included a cardiologist, psychologist, nurse, personal trainer, dietician, yoga and meditation teacher, and chef. For the first three months they met the heart patients three times a week for four hours each time: an hour for exercise, an hour for yoga and meditation, an hour for the support group, and an hour for a meal. Then, for nine months, they got together only once a week. For the second and third years the patients were left on their own. And then the results were measured. It turned out that 77 percent of the participants had changed their lifestyles so thoroughly that they had safely avoided the need for heart surgery. On average the 194 volunteers still practiced yoga and meditation for two hours a week. And they stuck remarkably well to the extreme diet: Only 8 percent of their calories came from fat. The Ornish program had cost only $7,000 per patient, while the bypass surgeries had cost an average of $46,000 apiece and the angioplasties had cost $31,000. When Mutual of Omaha did the math, it turned out that the Ornish program saved $30,000 a patient.

There's overwhelming evidence that Ornish's program inspires people to change profoundly. His studies were published by prestigious medical journals—the *Lancet*, the *American Journal of Cardiology*, and *The Journal of the American Medical Association*—that first subjected them to "peer review" by other scientists, who inspected the meticulousness of the studies' methods.

Even so, many people don't want to believe what he has accomplished. His ideas challenge their belief systems. His facts don't fit into their frames, so they don't seem to make sense. They're not heard or accepted. They're labeled as irrational, crazy, or stupid. People would walk out of the room when Ornish's results and methods were discussed at scientific conferences, even though scientists are supposed to be open to the free exchange of ideas.

Why does the Ornish program work? Because he's mastered the three keys to change.

KEY #1
Relate

Both the conventional approach and the Ornish approach start out well with the first key: The patient forms a relationship with a person—in both cases a "cardiologist"—who inspires hope. Ornish goes further, though. The patient's relationship isn't just with a single expert but with a team of experts—the trainer, yogi, chef, psychologist—and with a community of other patients who all strive to help one another.

KEY #2

Repeat

The second key to change is all about teaching, training, and learning. In the conventional approach, these things don't happen at all. Before they've been struck by the crisis of a heart attack or angina, people only get to visit with their physicians for brief appointments. "If you have eight minutes to see a new patient, you don't have time to talk about their diet or their exercise or their kid on heroin or the problems in their marriage or anything," says Ornish. "You basically have time to listen to the heart and lungs, write a prescription for Lipitor, and you're off to the next patient." The doctor doesn't have the time or training to teach patients how to diet or exercise or how to overcome their emotional and psychological struggles. There's much to learn in medical school about biology and pharmacology, and that doesn't leave much time for educating future physicians about nutrition or psychology. And teaching is an art of its own that doesn't come naturally to most people.

In the Ornish program, patients don't get much time with an expensive doctor either, but they spend many hours every week with other professionals who have the right training and beliefs to help them learn, practice, and master the new habits and skills that they'll need.

While the typical cardiologist doesn't believe patients can change their lifestyles, the yoga teacher believes patients can and will learn how to stretch and breath and meditate, the personal trainer is confident about getting them to walk for half an hour every day, and the chef knows that the food she prepares is so delicious that patients will get over the fact that it's vegetarian and they'll really enjoy eating it. The support group helps patients get into the habit of talking about their feelings with friends and finding hope from a sense of camaraderie and connectedness.

Ornish understands that habits such as smoking, drinking, overeating, overworking, and venting anger aren't really the "problems" for heart patients. The real problems are depression, loneliness, isolation, stress, unhappiness, powerlessness, anxiety, fear, hopelessness, and purposelessness. The underlying problems are psychological, emotional, and spiritual. Smoking, drinking, and overeating are "solutions" to these problems. Bad solutions, since they ultimately cause heart disease, but solutions nonetheless: They're effective ways of helping people get through the day. And when you're depressed or unhappy, that's a noble goal. "When you're depressed," Ornish says, "getting through the day is more important than living to eighty-six instead of eighty-five—even if you're eighty-five."

When Ornish was developing his program, smokers would warn him: "I have twenty friends in this pack of cigarettes. Are you going to take away my friends?" Yes, he has to. But what patients really need is to spend more time with human friends. They need to discover greater joy and purpose through greater interconnectedness with others. They need new "solutions" that don't have the side effect of worsening their heart disease. And that's exactly what they learn, practice, and master in the Ornish program.

KEY #3
Reframe

If people said that you could reverse a debilitating illness by stretching in weird positions or by hanging out more often with your buddies, you probably wouldn't believe them. If they said that you could get rid of awful, chronic pain on your own, without surgery or drugs, you might think they were nuts. If they asked you how to "live healthy," you might suggest going to a gym, but you might not recommend joining a church or synagogue, even though physical health actually depends so much on finding meaning and purpose in life through love, friendship, and community.

That's where the third key to change comes in. You need a relationship that helps you "reframe" and learn new ways of thinking. Ornish, like other proponents of preventative medicine, such as Dr. Andrew Weil, promotes a new system of beliefs—a new ideology about health and healing. He thinks patients should be active, not passive. Patients can be heroic, not helpless. Patients can take responsibility for their health rather than living irresponsibly. They can save themselves rather than counting on physicians to save them. Their physical health depends on their psychological, emotional, and spiritual health. The simple choices they make in their daily lives can promote their health just as much as a new drug or a new surgical technique or an expensive high-tech piece of equipment. They can deal with causes of illness rather than just seeking relief of symptoms.

When you're promoting a new way of thinking, you have a difficult job of persuading people. You have to "sell" it. Fortunately the techniques of salesmanship have been very well known for a very long time by many people (although this knowledge isn't taught at medical schools). It helps if you believe in what you're selling. It helps if you're passionate about it. It helps if you build rapport with your prospective customers and show that you care about them. It helps if you start out by speaking their language and by working within their existing beliefs. Even though Ornish himself was inspired by the Eastern philosophy of a swami, he knows that American doctors and patients have deep beliefs in science and Western medicine. He does as well, and he gains credibility from his credentials in that field—he is, after all, a professor at a top medical school. He often says "stretching and breathing exercises" and "relaxation skills" rather than "yoga and meditation." He talks about the importance of "interconnectedness" instead of using Eastern healing terminology such as Chi, Prana, or Shakti.

It's easier to sell something once you prove that it works. The biggest selling point of the Ornish program is the 91 percent decrease in the frequency of chest pains in one month. "These rapid improvements are a powerful motivator," Ornish says. "When people who have had so much chest pain that they can't work, or make love, or even walk across the street without intense suffering find that they are able to do all those things without pain in only a few weeks, then they often say, 'These are choices worth making.'"

Other heart doctors try to motivate patients to change by summoning "the fear of death," but that doesn't help when patients are demoralized. If they're in denial, they'll avoid thinking about the problem. And telling people who are depressed that they can live longer if they make difficult changes doesn't inspire them. "Who wants to live longer when you're in chronic emotional pain?" Ornish asks. So, instead of the "fear of death," Ornish's sales pitch is "the joy of living"—his teams convince patients that they can not only live longer but also feel better. Patients can look forward to enjoying the things that make daily life pleasurable. And within one month, they're feeling the joy.

Psych Concept #3
Short-term Wins

The Ornish program relies on what John Kotter, a professor at Harvard Business School who has spent decades studying leadership and change in corporations, calls the importance of "short-term wins." Kotter says it's always vital to identify, achieve, and celebrate some quick, positive results for the emotional lifts they provide. When organizations of all kinds try to change the habitual ways their members think, feel, and act, they need "victories that nourish faith in the change effort, emotionally reward the hard workers, keep the critics at bay, and build momentum," Kotter says. "Without sufficient wins that are visible, timely, unambiguous, and meaningful to others, change efforts invariably run into serious problems."

The idea may seem weirdly paradoxical, but the Ornish program shows that radical, sweeping, comprehensive changes are sometimes easier for people than small, incremental ones. Ornish says that people who make moderate changes in their diets get the worst of both worlds: They feel deprived and hungry because they aren't eating everything they want, but they aren't making big enough changes to see an improvement in how they feel, or in measurements such as weight, blood pressure, and cholesterol.

The "short-term wins" inspire hope for Ornish's patients, encouraging the belief that they can change and the expectation that they will change. When they see the results from their new habits and skills, then they start to change how they think. That's how belief systems ultimately shift.

The technocrats who run Western industrialized societies—not only the doctors and scientists, but also the engineers, lawyers, and corporate managers—pride themselves on their disciplined, analytical thinking, and they're used to simply telling others what to do. Often they don't realize the need for emotional persuasion. But change is about selling, not telling. It's about teaching as well as preaching. Instead of complaining that people don't follow your orders, you need to start training them in new skills.

•

Now in the fourth decade of his personal quest, Ornish is finally beginning to change the beliefs of the people who run America's health care establishment. In 2005 the commissioners of Medicare, the federal government's health insurer, voted to cover the costs of his program, which means that millions of heart patients who aren't as wealthy as Dick Cheney can also have teams of experts there to help them live in a healthier way.

CHANGE 101

Cheat Sheet #1

(Crib notes on the theory so far)

CASE STUDY: HEART PATIENTS

CONVENTIONAL STRATEGY OF "THE THREE Fs": FACTS, FEAR, AND FORCE

Doctors try to motivate the patient with the facts of the medical diagnosis, play on the patient's fear of dying, and rely on the force of their own professional authority.

Why This Fails

DENIAL: Dying is too scary to think about, so the patient puts up psychological self-defenses and reverts to an unhealthy lifestyle.

FRAMES: In the conceptual framework of Western medicine, the patients, who are hopeless and passive, need to be saved by the doctors, who are heroic. Both parties believe that surgery and drugs can restore health. They don't accept the idea that patients can restore their own health by how they live on a daily basis going forward.

THE CHANGE STRATEGY OF THE THREE Rs

KEY #1 (RELATE): Patients form new, emotional relationships with one another and with a team of professionals—including a cardiologist, psychologist, personal trainer, chef, and yoga/meditation instructor—who fervently believe patients can change.

Psych Concept: Short-term Wins. The rapid improvement in the patients' health—dramatic results after just one month—helps to "sell" the patients on the program and inspire them to stick with it even though it's a very demanding change.

KEY #2 (REPEAT): The team helps patients learn, practice, and master new habits and skills—such as diet, exercise, yoga, meditation, and social connectedness—for overcoming the underlying physiological, psychological, emotional, and spiritual aspects of their disease.

KEY #3 (REFRAME): Ultimately patients learn to take responsibility for their own health through their daily lifestyles rather than by relying on physicians to cure them.

PSYCH CONCEPTS (SO FAR)

1. Frames
2. Denial and other psychological self-defenses
3. Short-term wins

CASE STUDY:

Criminals

This chapter is going to build up our theory of change by looking in closer detail at how the Delancey Street program transforms chronically drug-addicted felons into sober, productive, law-abiding citizens. But first, to introduce you to one of the key concepts behind the success of Delancey, I'm going to tell a true story about a few people I know and like who work in the corporate world. Just so there's absolutely no confusion, let me make it very clear that they're not addicts or convicted criminals.

Psych Concept #4
The Power of Community and Culture

In 1996, when he was thirty-one years old, David Risher was working as a marketing executive at Microsoft's headquarters in the suburbs of Seattle. His colleagues respected his intelligence and liked his calm, soft-spoken, gracious manner. They thought he could become one of the top people there at the world's wealthiest and most successful company. Still, Risher was curious enough to interview for a job at a small company that had been around for only a year and was losing money. It was called Amazon.com, and its founder, Jeff Bezos, had been one of Risher's classmates at Princeton University. They hadn't known each other in college, which seemed odd, since Princeton is a small school and nearly all the students live in the dormitories on campus. It turned out that they had belonged to the same "eating club," an old house where 150 members hung out and threw parties and gathered for three meals a day in a large dining room. Though Risher had been the club's president, he hadn't known Bezos. That was probably because Bezos spent so much of his time down the street at the campus's computer center. Bezos graduated with a 4.2 grade point average in his major, electrical engineering and computer science, meaning that he received mostly A-pluses, which count as 4.3 and are rarely awarded.

When Risher went for his job interview, Amazon was renting office space in an old brick building on Seattle's skid row, a dismal block with a needle exchange, a defunct pawnshop, a grocery store with barren shelves, and an outreach service for troubled youths. Inside, the offices looked cheap. Bezos believed in frugality. He hated spending cash on things that didn't seem to matter. Even though he had made a lot of money working on Wall Street in his twenties, he drove a Honda and lived in a small apartment. At Amazon he built his own makeshift desk by buying a cheap wooden door at Home Depot to serve as the work surface and sawing off two-by-fours for the legs. His employees followed his example and built their own desks the same way.

When Risher entered Bezos's office, he saw a white board on the wall. Bezos had scribbled two hundred marketing ideas that Amazon could pursue.

"Prioritize this," Bezos said, handing him a magic marker. Bezos wanted him to rank the ideas from one to two hundred.

Risher was up for the challenge. The two men realized that they were very much alike: They were both so compulsively analytical that it was kind of comical. Risher's wife made fun of his penchant for "numbering things." Bezos *talked* in ranked lists. He liked to enumerate the criteria, in order of importance, for every decision he made—even why he married his wife MacKenzie. The number one reason for that particular choice: He wanted someone inventive and resourceful enough to get him out of a Third World prison.

During his visit Risher met fifteen of Amazon's thirty employees. "I was blown away because everyone was super-smart," he recalls. How had Bezos recruited such a bright team? Later, over dinner, Bezos told him, "I'd rather interview fifty people and not hire anyone than hire the wrong person."

Bezos had followed this philosophy from the company's

earliest days. In 1995, when Amazon was preparing to launch its website and begin selling books, Bezos's colleagues urged him to hire a bunch of people and do it fast. They would bring in one job candidate after another after another, but Bezos refused to hire any of them. His behavior was perplexing. The company was growing quickly and they desperately needed to hire. "Our attitude was that we need a body in here," says Paul Barton-Davis, who was Amazon's third employee. But Bezos had a very particular idea of who he wanted. He was looking for people who were frugal and resourceful and loved to analyze information and try new things and take big risks—people like *himself*.

Back when hardly anyone had ever heard of Amazon, a tiny start-up company that hadn't yet sold a dollar's worth of stuff, it was ridiculously difficult to get a job there, even if you had inside connections. Even when you applied for a job answering the phones in the customer service department, Bezos's colleagues would compile a one-hundred-page dossier about you. One of the early employees, Eric Dillon, referred four of his friends, and Bezos wouldn't hire any of them. "It was brutal," Dillon says.

When Dave Risher decided to accept Bezos's offer and go work for Amazon, his peers at Microsoft were stunned. They were all paid partly in company stock that was rising rapidly at the time, and they stood to make fortunes if they hung around for just a few years. "In '96 *nobody* left Microsoft to go to another company," Risher says. "When people left Microsoft, it was to retire."

Risher was summoned to meet with Steve Ballmer, Microsoft's number two executive—a big, bald man with a booming voice and a personality that can be forceful and intimidating. Then he met with Bill Gates, the company's cofounder and number one executive and the world's richest and most powerful businessperson. "They said I was the stupidest guy they ever met," Risher recalls. It wasn't just that Risher was walking away from millions of dollars. Ballmer, Gates, and thousands of others at Microsoft shared an ideology. They believed that Microsoft was the most important and exciting place to work. The fact that a promising executive would want to work for someone else simply didn't fit their frame, so they dismissed it as stupid.

In 1996, Amazon brought in $16 million in revenue. Three years later, its annual revenues had gone up a hundredfold to $1.6 billion. By its tenth anniversary, the figure surpassed $8 billion. What's really fascinating is that the company's "culture"—its collective "personality," or the values, myths, habits, practices, and belief systems of its people—remained pretty much the same even as thousands upon thousands of new recruits came on to the payroll. Ten years into its life as a company, when Amazon had twelve thousand employees, you could walk the halls and still see people sitting at desks built from doors, and you could overhear them talking about the five top reasons, in order, why they picked a certain mountain in the Cascades for the hiking trip they had planned for the coming weekend.

Not long after he hired Risher, Amazon had become too large for Bezos himself to continue his practice of interviewing and approving all the new hires. But by then he didn't have to do so any longer. The first few dozen people create a culture that's self-perpetuating. Their personalities make up a company's cultural DNA, the genetic code that replicates again and again. Bezos hires a bunch of people, like Risher, who in turn hire many others. The newcomers arrive at a place that already has its own set of well-defined values, beliefs, practices, skills, quirks, and even delusions. Since they depend on Amazon for their livelihoods, they have a strong incentive to model their behavior on the people around them, especially the stars and the higher-ups. The newcomers try hard to fit in. If they can't fit in, they quit. If they fit in particularly well, they rise and become role models for the newer hires. The overall effect is that the culture created by Bezos and Barton-Davis and Risher is *sticky*.

"Cultures are these fantastic things," Bezos told me around the time of Amazon's tenth anniversary. "Cultures are not so much planned as they evolve from that early set of people. Once a corporate culture is formed, it tends to be extremely stable. It stays around. It ends up building on itself."

Cultures stuck for *decades* at a number of well-known companies, such as Microsoft, General Motors, and IBM, but my all-time favorite example is Anheuser-Busch, the company that sells about half the beer consumed in the United States, including the best-selling brand, Budweiser. Busch's executives were very well paid, and they could afford the most expensive wines from France and California, but they always kept kegs of Bud on tap in their beautiful homes in the suburbs of St. Louis. When they traveled on business to New York, they went to lunch at the fanciest restaurants, such as Le Cirque, but their assistants called ahead to make sure they would be served Bud, which wasn't typically on the menus. When the executives arrived, six-packs of longnecks would be waiting in silver ice buckets on their tables, as if Bud were what everyone drank there.

When the Busch boys attended Oktoberfest in Munich, they would sample the most acclaimed German beers, and still, they'd say to one another that the award winners just didn't taste as good as Bud. Even after more intensely flavorful "microbrews" became popular throughout the United States, the Busch people still told one another that their mass-produced, cheaper, more watery Bud had the most appealing taste.

If you left another company and became an executive at Anheuser-Busch, you'd have to act "as if" you felt Bud was really the best beer, and after you acted that way for a long enough time, you wouldn't have to fake it anymore. You would actually start to believe it yourself. That's how persistent and influential a company's culture can be.

If you really wanted to test the full power of culture and community, if you wanted to push it to the utmost limits, here's an experiment you could try: You could take a bunch of drug-addicted, violent, unskilled, psychopathic criminals and hire them to work at an entrepreneurial company with a reputation for customer service. And you could use this experience to reshape them into law-abiding, sober, peaceful, caring, cooperative, skilled workers striving to achieve the American Dream. That's exactly what Dr. Mimi Silbert has done for thirty-five years at Delancey Street.

·

Normally when I go to interview corporate executives in the San Francisco Bay Area—at Google or Yahoo, for example—I wear jeans and sneakers. I don't worry if I haven't shaved in a couple of days or if my hair is somewhat disheveled or my shirt is wrinkled and untucked. And I look as if I belong at a Silicon Valley company. But when I was getting ready to interview Mimi Silbert, I made sure to put on my best dark suit, a freshly pressed shirt, and polished dress shoes. I was clean shaven and combed. I knew that the ex-convicts at Delancey would be neatly dressed and groomed, and I didn't want to feel embarrassed for looking slovenly.

When I arrived at the Delancey Street Restaurant in the middle of the afternoon, I was greeted by an African American waiter who was as large as a linebacker. He was so courteous and polished that he could have been working at the Ritz. He took me to a private dining room overlooking the bay and brought a tray of fresh fruit and cheese that easily could have fed a dozen hungry people.

Silbert burst in, followed by her dog, Amnesty. Like Jeff Bezos, Mimi Silbert exudes energy and laughs uproariously every few moments. Through two hours of conversation, she only rarely mentioned any terms that you might hear in an academic course or read in a psychology book. Even though she studied existentialism in

Paris with the famed philosopher Jean-Paul Sartre and earned doc-torates in philosophy and criminology from the University of Cali-fornia at Berkeley, where she worked as a professor for a brief time, Silbert expresses disdain for theory. The way she describes it, three of the most influential ideas behind the psychology of Delancey Street were inspired by experiences in her life rather than theoriz-ing in the academy.

Her first formative experience was growing up in a poor immi-grant family and pursuing the American Dream. She was the only child of Eastern European Jewish immigrant parents who spoke Yiddish with her at home. They lived very close to her entire ex-tended family—grandparents, aunts, uncles, and cousins—in a small, tight-knit immigrant community in Boston. It was the kind of place where everyone knew one another and they looked out for and took care of one another. When children misbehaved, family members or neighbors caught them and made sure their parents heard about it. The sense of community instilled the notions of ac-countability and responsibility.

Silbert's extended family strived to join the middle class as some of their former neighbors had done. As a child she learned the work ethic by filling in as a soda jerk in her father's corner drugstore. The whole clan prospered, and when she was twelve they moved from small rental apartments in the "ghetto" to little houses they bought in the suburbs.

Silbert was a cheerleader as a teenager. Her family put such a strong emphasis on education that she stayed in school until she earned two PhDs. Then she taught at Berkeley while also working as a therapist. By her late twenties she had married and given birth to twin sons. End the story there and it would be uplifting but conventional, just one of millions of tales of immigrants who achieved upward mobility by helping one another, learning the culture of their new country, believing in education, and working hard.

But that's not where the story ends. While she was a professor and a therapist, Silbert also worked as a consultant to state prisons and trained parole officers. "It didn't take me long to realize that everything we did with the prison population was wrong," she says. The problem wasn't that prisoners had psychological disorders or that they were psychopaths. The real issue was that they were poor. "It was not a matter of therapy," she says. "The bulk of people filling up the state prisons are just the underclass. It is primarily poor people. They're people who have no idea how the American middle-class system works. It's a different culture, language, and attitude. It became clear to me that they needed to learn what I had learned."

The problem was that families had remained stuck in the under-class. Millions of poor people had become demoralized. They had lost the hope of moving up in American society. Generation after generation after generation remained poor and relied on financial assistance from the government, reinforcing the belief that they were hopeless and powerless.

"We're a country based on mobility," Silbert says. "But in 200 years we've already lost mobility for a huge section of the population. They receive welfare. They're not needed. They're essentially powerless in society, and it's the most corrupting thing I know. Because they live at the bottom of things, they're always passive recipients. People say that power corrupts. I can't say strongly enough how much powerlessness corrupts."

KEY #1

Relate

To overcome their demoralization, the chronically poor needed a new relationship to inspire new hope and help them learn new skills and new ways of thinking. Silbert's breakthrough idea was that the new underclass could learn exactly the way she had learned as a child in a Boston ghetto in the forties and fifties. Delancey Street would simulate the kind of extended family or close-knit immigrant neighborhood where she had picked up the habits, practices, and beliefs that had enabled her to succeed. She would put them in "a community culture based on old-fashioned American values."

Silbert's second enlightening experience came from working as a therapist in private practice. When she conducted sessions with clients, she was the one who learned from the experience. When her clients thanked her for helping them, *she* was the one who felt better. Therapy was astonishingly therapeutic *for the therapist.* Whether or not her clients actually learned anything or felt any better, Silbert knew for sure that she had. "Everybody needs to be *me,*" she thought. And this sparked another powerful idea: At Delancey the convicts could develop self-respect from helping one another, even though their own knowledge and skills were limited. If someone knew how to read at the sixth-grade level, he could teach someone else who hadn't gotten beyond the second-grade level. That student, in turn, could teach another skill to someone else. The idea is called "each one, teach one."

Silbert's third insight came from working as a consultant to fifty police departments. Her job was to help train new recruits to become police officers. Since cops are often drawn into dangerous encounters that require quick action, their best way to prepare is by "role-playing"—simulating situations and repeating the proper behavior until it becomes instinctive, until they can do the right thing in a split second "without thinking."

If we train civilians to think, feel, and act like cops, then why can't we *train* criminals to think, feel, and act like lawful citizens? If psychopaths acted "as if" they cared about other people, would they really start to care? And what if criminals trained *one another* instead of having professionals train them?

•

Those were Mimi Silbert's inspirations for Delancey Street. Now let's look at her ideas in action:

Criminals choose to live at Delancey when judges offer the program as an alternative to serving time in prison. At first, many offenders see Delancey as a "get out of jail free" pass. They're still thinking within their longtime frame—their "criminal mind"—so they think that Delancey is a scam that they're shrewdly exploiting. Instead of submitting to prison guards and parole officers who love to "kick their butts," they're scheming to get away with "one more con" by taking advantage of San Francisco liberals who like to "kiss their butts." They don't go to Delancey believing or expecting that they can change how they live.

Look at a few typical examples:

Deborah was a heroin addict at twelve, a street prostitute at thirteen. She dropped out of the ninth grade. Her baby drowned in the bathtub while she was taking a heroin fix. She spent five years in prison. She went through many programs and hospitals, playing what she called "the cure game," but she knew she would always be an addict. She tried to kill herself three times. Then, "to beat a prison case," she went to Delancey.

Christina was a junkie and hadn't been out of jail for longer than three months at a time since she was twelve. She chose Delancey instead of serving two consecutive sentences of twenty-five years to life for robbery and violence.

Gerald has a scar on his neck from the 102 stitches he received after a knife fight at Folsom Prison. He had been incarcerated three times, for a total of fifteen years, for armed robbery and other felonies. One time he was sent back to prison after only a month of freedom. He came to Delancey as a way of getting out of a twenty-year prison sentence for drug crimes. Delancey requires a commitment of only two years. The decision was easy.

The pimps, prostitutes, thieves, drug lords and other gangsters who arrive at Delancey are usually addicts. At one point Delancey did a formal survey and found that 85 percent of its incoming residents were heroin addicts for an average of ten years. More than 40 percent were alcoholics. (The numbers add up to more than 100 percent because 60 percent abused more than one substance.) Typically they were hooked since adolescence or even childhood. "Some took alcohol to school in milk cartons in the second grade," Silbert says.

KEY #2
Repeat

Learning and practicing, day after day, how to live without threats, violence, drugs, or alcohol, and how to dress, walk, talk, and act like a middle-class citizen.

When new recruits arrive at Delancey's complex in San Francisco, the first thing they have to do is overcome their addictions. The rule that no one can use drugs or consume alcohol starts from day one. There's no methadone for heroin addicts. They have to quit "cold turkey." They're put on living room couches and served homemade chicken soup for the bad flu that results. Alcoholics have a harder time, actually—you can die from alcohol withdrawal—so they're sent to a local hospital, always accompanied by longtime Delancey residents to make sure they don't run away.

"From now on, you're an ex-dope fiend," Silbert tells the Delancey newcomers.

"The problem of drugs is not really physical," she explained to me. "The real issue is: How do you make your life work without drugs or hatred? We don't use the language of drug programs that says you're 'sick' or 'in recovery.' Our environment is not a therapeutic environment. It's a learning environment." They don't bother exploring the particular reasons why anyone was a junkie or a drunk or a gangster: "Cause is irrelevant. We don't ask why. We know you can do it. Don't look for the cause; just know that impossible change is possible. Therapy starts on the inside, going for self-knowledge, which doesn't always change behavior. Self-knowledge is a wonderful gift, but if you're a self-destructive person and your life doesn't work, you have to start from the outside in—how you dress, how you walk, how you speak. At Delancey you spend one year learning an entirely new *outside*."

Those are the first things that the newcomers are taught by the residents who've been there longer—how to dress, walk, speak, and groom themselves as if they were part of the middle class rather than the underclass.

KEY #3
Reframe

The newcomers' arrival at Delancey's "Intake Department" is known as "immigration." They're told to think of themselves as members of a large extended family in a tight-knit community of immigrants who have to help one another if they are going to learn the ways of their new country and survive there. That country is the belief system of the prosperous, peaceful bourgeoisie, which Delancey embraces and embodies in microcosm.

Delancey is also modeled on a corporation. It's a hierarchical organization where performance and experience are the ways to move up. The only people who don't have job titles are the immigrants, who are assigned to grubby maintenance work. While they're living in open, communal quarters and spending their days pushing brooms, they see that residents who've been there longer live in private rooms and hold more prestigious positions. The veterans have risen to the middle (working as waiters or chefs or movers) or the top (running the restaurant or the moving business, which have many workers and take in millions of dollars of revenue every year).

MORE OF KEY #1
Relate

Delancey divides the immigrants into small groups, which function like immediate families within the extended family. Everyone is assigned to a group of ten people, all the same sex, and they share a barracks-style dormitory space. These small cells are the only aspect of Delancey that *isn't* hierarchical. They're called *minyans* after the Jewish tradition that ten members of a congregation may join together and hold a prayer service without the leadership of a formally educated and ordained rabbi. Aside from Silbert, there aren't any trained professionals at Delancey. There are no psychiatrists, psychologists, therapists, social workers, or parole officers. "You can't have a healthy culture of change if there's a 'we' and a 'they.' " Beside herself, there are only criminals and drug addicts, and they're put into self-directed teams. "The ten people become the rabbi," Silbert says.

Nine of the members are "immigrants." The tenth person, who serves as the leader, is a longer-time resident who has assimilated to the Delancey culture. The leader is the first among equals; there's no hierarchy in the group. The idea is that all ten are responsible for and accountable to one another. Their group meetings, held three times a week, can be loud and acrimonious. "When a minyan leader yells at you, as a parent would, he talks to everyone else, too," Silbert says. The entire group shares the blame for the failings of any one of its members. "By not caring, the others are equally responsible." If one person breaks a rule—stealing someone else's possessions, for example, even if it's just a T-shirt—the others are supposed to report it. "Minyans break the 'code of silence' of the streets, where no one talks," Silbert says.

If your peers catch you breaking the rules—and there's nowhere to hide, since the residents are constantly together—you'll be punished. The big taboos—drugs, alcohol, threats, and violence—get you thrown out of Delancey without question, but lesser transgressions get you extra dishwashing, the all-purpose disciplinary action.

You might be sentenced to an extra hour or an extra month's worth depending on the circumstances. But the most powerful punishment is the disapproval of the community.

The minyan leader serves as an initial role model for the other members. "We don't start with asking people to take responsibility for themselves," Silbert says. "They don't have it yet. They just feel victimized. We develop change by asking people to see it in someone else."

The minyan meetings aren't a forum for people to talk about themselves and their own feelings. They're about criticizing others unsparingly, and harshly if necessary, for their mistakes, flaws, failures, and weaknesses. "What's critical is the constant feedback of your peers," Silbert says. "We do 'groups' but we don't do 'therapy groups.' A group is where everybody talks to you about what they see in you. If one person says something critical to you, you can say, 'Screw him.' If everybody says it, you realize, 'That's the impact I have on people, whether I intend it or not, and I have to change.' See, that's peer pressure, ultimately, in any family."

People are blind to their own faults—denial, denial, denial—but their flaws are easily seen by everyone around them. Silbert's brilliant way of combating denial is to eschew the whole idea of "therapy" and rely on peer pressure in a small, self-contained society that has a very strong culture. Another ingenious idea is having the immigrants learn to take responsibility for themselves by first asking them to take responsibility for other people.

The problem with asking criminals to care about other people is that they don't feel anything, at least not at first. They're not empathic. Early in life they learned *not* to care, which is a necessary form of psychological self-defense when you're trapped in a culture of violence, poverty, hopelessness, and early death. "People don't understand what it's like to be a third-generation criminal," Silbert says. "The only way to survive is to not give a damn. And drugs are a good way, because they stop you from feeling."

Silbert doesn't expect the immigrants to care for each other, at least not at first. She asks them to act "as if" they care. Alcoholics Anonymous relies on the same approach, telling new members, "Fake it until you make it."

Psych Concept #5
Acting As If

It's obvious that what we believe and what we feel influences how we act. That's common sense. But the equation works in the other direction as well: *How we act influences what we believe and what we feel.* That's one of the most counterintuitive yet powerful principles of modern psychology.

This same concept is actually one of the most important foundations of ancient religious practices. In both the Jewish and Christian traditions "inner faith and outer action likewise feed each other," writes David Myers, who studies the intersection of psychology and spirituality as a professor at the aptly named Hope College. "Throughout the Old and New Testaments, faith is seen as nurtured by obedient action. For example, in the Old Testament the Hebrew word for 'know' is usually a verb, designating something one does. To know love, one must not only know about love, one must act lovingly. Philosophers and theologians note how faith grows as people act on what little faith they have. Rather than insist that people believe before they pray, Talmudic scholars would tell rabbis, get them to pray and their belief will grow."

One way to grasp this idea is to think of a couple that decides to adopt a pet. Let's say the wife really wants a dog but the husband resists the idea—he has never had pets and he isn't naturally drawn to them. At first he grumbles about having to feed or walk the dog. Still, after several months of actively taking care of Fido, he'll probably develop a real affection for the furry creature. The *act* of caring ultimately instills the *emotion* of care.

If you grew up in a violent subculture where many people were killed at tragically young ages, and your psychological self-defense mechanism was to avoid caring for others, and you never learned how to care for people, then you never really experienced what caring feels like. It's a new habit or skill that you need to learn, practice, and master (Key #2), and once you do, then a whole new way of thinking begins to make sense (Key #3). The "acting as if" concept explains why *repetition* helps to promote *reframing*. Repeated personal experience over a long time is what conditions our gut-level emotions and strongly held beliefs. It takes new firsthand experiences, repeated over and over and over again, to begin to change our "frames." Reframing isn't something that happens just by hearing another person explain a new way of looking at things. You have to *do* things a new way before you can *think* in a new way.

"Acting as if" isn't easy. Many people don't make it through Delancey Street. Around one third of the immigrants drop out or get kicked out of the program within the first few months. They return to state prisons, and in many cases, they realize that's where they would rather be. "The horror of prison is that it becomes comfortable," Silbert says. "Repeat offenders always have friends to come home to. And they very quickly learn to live by the rules of prison society—hatred, bigotry, gangs. The very rules that prevent you from living on the outside."

But most immigrants stay at Delancey because the first few weeks open them to the astonishing possibility that their lives could take a different course. They see that they have been able to live without drugs and violence, if only for a short time. Silbert, like Ornish, recognizes the power of "short-term wins" for inspiring change. The Delancey immigrants see the longer-time residents—people *just like themselves*—who've lasted for two, three, or four years at Delancey and now run its profitable businesses and are treated respectfully by outsiders.

In the beginning the immigrants are still thinking with their criminal minds, so the situation still doesn't make much sense to them. The tangible facts don't fit their frames. They've long believed that the only way for people like themselves to become powerful and prosperous is by dealing drugs, so some convince themselves that Delancey must be a scam, an elaborate cover for a drug operation. Deborah stayed at Delancey because she believed "there must be something 'dirty' going on," and she wanted to get in on the action.

So they spend that first year pushing a broom or a mop and being told to pretend they care about the others there even though they're surrounded by the kinds of people they've always hated. The Delancey population has roughly even numbers of blacks, whites, and Latinos who've mostly been members of ethnic or racial gangs. Would-be Nazis covered with swastika tattoos live alongside Silbert, whose family members were sent to the Nazi death camps. The "peer feedback" she gives them is: "Look in the mirror. I've got to tell you, you're not what Hitler meant by a master race."

What's fascinating is that even while she's humiliating these immigrants, Silbert doesn't bother to argue about their beliefs. "There's a rationale for everything," she says, "even gratuitous violence and crime if you follow their version of reality." She can't appeal to their conscience because they've lived without conscience. "In the early years," she says, "the average Delancey Street person was a first-generation criminal, and I could say: 'This is what your mother scrubbed toilets for?' You could connect to a *feeling*. That's not true anymore. Now their grandparents write them saying, 'Come back to the gang, sell drugs, and take revenge.' The gang mentality is based on vengeance. Prisons in California are controlled by gangs, and you have to hurt people if you want to be a part of the gang. This is a population who are considered 'psychopaths' or 'sociopaths.' They feel no guilt. They have no conscience in the traditional sense."

The immigrants don't feel any remorse about what they've done in the past, and Silbert doesn't ask them to, at least not at first. Delancey keeps them busy pushing that broom and being taught to read and write by other residents, and in turn teaching others whatever useful skills they possess, and practicing new ways to walk and talk, and acting "as if" they care for people around them. "We don't let them mope," Silbert says. "We keep them busy. Don't talk about

the streets. We're busy; we've got things to do. People need you."
Then a very strange thing starts to happen at some point during
that first brutally difficult year. "Every success every minute begins
to show them their strengths," Silbert says. "And all of a sudden the
act 'as if' becomes real."

MORE OF KEY #3
Reframe

When criminals grasp that they *can* live without drugs, violence, or
cruelty, when they realize that they *have* already lived that way for
nearly a year, this new knowledge becomes extraordinary difficult
to deal with. When they begin to have real feelings for the people
around them, they're overwhelmed by guilt for how they treated
people earlier in their lives. These criminals are quickly overtaken
by remorse and self-hatred. "They've been diagnosed as 'psychopaths,' but they're actually consumed and paralyzed by guilt," Silbert says. That's when Delancey finally asks them to feel bad about
their histories. "This great new self overlays the old self," says Silbert, "and you need to dissipate the guilt of everything you've
done."

Many religions hold rituals of repentance, and Delancey's own
ecumenical ceremony is known as "Dissipation." During a long
weekend, as many as eighteen residents take turns spending hours
telling their life stories. "We want the facts of your story but we
need the emotions," Silbert says. "You look at every single thing you
did and feel sorry. Let yourself feel it. In the early years of Delancey
Street, Dissipation was the first time they had cried since they were

children. Now, for many, it's the first time they've ever cried. It's the first time they've had feelings. You have an audience, and people say to you: 'That's not you anymore. That's who you used to be.' You've 'balanced the scales' some and you're not bad. Then you can face it. Forgiveness is tortuous if you're not ready to forgive yourself."

"Balancing the scales" is a crucial idea at Delancey. Silbert tells the criminals: "You've done a lot of horrible things, and you can't undo them, but you can do good things until one day the scales will tip." When she talks with me, she explains her moral calculus: "All of us rise to the best of ourselves and sink to the worst of ourselves. I'm really big on the idea that nothing is either/or. You're not either good or bad. You're not either healthy or sick. Every day you don't do the right thing, then *that day* you're an asshole. There's no reaching the 'healthy way.' You choose it by doing it.

"I purposefully avoid theory if I can," she says, "but I studied under Sartre, existentialist theory, for a minute, and that's what this is. It's all about replacing determinism with the concept of choice, self-respect, and control of your own life. I also try to teach that there actually are rights and wrongs. If you do something good, you should feel good about it, and if you do something wrong, you've got to press the pause button and say, 'Oh, shit.' You should admit to it and fix it. We're dealing with people who've taken a lot from society, and they need to make restitution. We do endless volunteering with kids, seniors, AIDS foundations, and on and on. I say: 'You've got to be a more responsible citizen than anyone else when you're here and when you graduate because you're 'balancing the scales.' "

Psych Concept #6

Recasting a Life's Story

Even though change is a vital part of life, people crave a feeling of consistency and continuity. We all have a sense of who we are as individuals, and we like to think that our identities, our cherished senses of self—our core conceptions of "this is who I am"—remain stable over time. We like to believe: "I'm the same person now that I always was." I'm Alan, and even though I've grown, matured, and learned a lot in forty-one years, I like to think that there's some essential "Alan-ness" that you can see in the home movies of my childhood birthday parties and will remain the same even when I'm at my grandchildren's birthday parties.

But the sense of self is threatened by any major change in the deep-rooted patterns of how we think, feel, and act, even a tremendously positive change such as leaving behind a life of crime and addiction. A change-in-progress demands new explanations for a past that's now cast in a darker light. The New Self has to come to terms with the Old Self. If it turns out that you can live as a sober, responsible, peaceful, and productive member of society, then why didn't you live that way in the first place? Even if your past life involved nothing you should feel guilty about, nothing immoral or illegal, it still becomes much more difficult to look back with self-respect. If it turns out that you *could* lose an impressive amount of weight and become remarkably slender and fit, that you weren't a victim of some overpowering "fat gene" that scientists have yet to decode, then why were you obese for so many of your prime years? If you *could* overcome heart disease by changing your lifestyle, then why did you put yourself through the trauma of bypass surgery a few years earlier? If you *could* revamp your company and make it thriving and profitable again, then how do you justify the years when it lost millions of dollars? One of the reasons we resist change, unconsciously at least, is that it invalidates years of earlier behavior.

While this is an unconscious barrier to change, there's also a solution that operates outside of our awareness. Psychologists now theorize that there isn't some immutable "self" that defines who you are and always will be; instead, "we constantly construct and reconstruct our selves," writes Jerome Bruner, a cognitive scientist at New York University. And we do it by the stories that we tell about our lives. We're constantly rewriting our autobiographies in our own minds to make better sense of our past and present and our hopes and plans for the future. We rather conveniently forget certain facts and details and interpret others in entirely new ways. Usually we're not aware that this is what we're doing.

Here's an example: During my college years, when I majored in political theory, I considered myself a "libertarian" and voted for Ronald Reagan in the presidential election. But by my late thirties, I considered myself a "liberal" or "progressive" and voted for Al Gore. Now if you told those facts to independent critics, they'd probably say that I had gone through a profound change in my political leanings—from Republican to Democrat, from far right to center-left. But I would argue that my thinking had simply evolved in a logical way—I still cherished civil liberties and appreciated the power of the free market but I had come to realize the importance of government regulation and action on crucial issues such as environmental protection. In my mind there was a compelling internal logic and clear direction to my political history. Other people might say I had flipped sides. Maybe they'd be correct. But it's difficult for me to look back and think that I spent years fervently advocating a political ideology that would now embarrass me in front of most of my friends. No one likes to reminisce and say, "Gee, what was I thinking?" I'd rather tell myself that I was smart about politics in my earlier years, and I've become even smarter about it as I've aged and matured.

Sometimes what keeps a person from going through with a change is the inability to rewrite an autobiography. My father, for example, who's a professor of civil engineering, once thought about switching careers in midlife and enrolling in law school. He loved reading legal thrillers, and he was enamored of the courtroom attorneys he worked with when he occasionally testified as an expert witness at a trial or appeared in front of a city planning commission. He would have loved being one of them. But how would he explain giving up a coveted, tenured faculty position and becoming a first-year graduate student once again? Could he bring himself to tell other people—and to tell *himself*—that his earlier career had been some kind of mistake? That he really should have become a lawyer instead of an engineer in the first place? That three decades of his professional life had been misdirected? To make the switch, he would have needed to come up with a new story—not just to satisfy other people, but also to satisfy himself and to cast his life's story in a new, coherent form. He could have said that he always thrived on challenge and that he needed the stimulation of a new world to conquer. He could have come up with any number of compelling explanations that made new sense of his autobiography. But he didn't. At sixty-eight, he's still a professor of engineering.

Delancey Street doesn't just teach moral principles. It teaches how to live in capitalist society. Silbert is an insider among San Francisco's corporate elite: She's a close friend of Howard Lester, the longtime head of the Pottery Barn, and Mickey Drexler, the former chief of The Gap, which has its headquarters a few blocks down from Delancey on the waterfront. It's obvious why they admire her accomplishments in business: "At Delancey we're running companies with people who didn't know how to do anything and had failed at everything in their lives," Silbert says, laughing.

Delancey began when John Maher, an ex-convict, approached Silbert for help in writing a grant proposal for federal money. She refused. Instead she convinced him that his program should be self-supporting, and she became its cofounder. Delancey has never taken money from the government. Even though it does receive some donations from Silbert's corporate friends, such as Gap clothing, the program depends primarily on the profitability of its businesses, which are run and staffed entirely by its own residents. "We live on the edge," Silbert says. "We purposefully set it up so at any time we can fail. I say, 'If we go down, I will take my degrees and earn several hundred dollars an hour, and you will go to shit.' It's hard for people to understand that they're needed and respected and accountable. It's best taught through other people. As you move up here, you have responsibility for an increasing number of people."

While Delancey is an entrepreneurial company in its own right and a training academy for future workers and managers in American capitalism, it also resembles a commune in many ways. The Delancey people don't just work together. They *live* together. No one at Delancey receives a salary, not even Silbert. The revenues from the businesses belong to the community, which provides food, clothing, and housing for the residents. Silbert was influenced by a visit to a kibbutz, an Israeli communal farm. But she prefers the metaphor of Delancey as a large extended family.

Delancey, like Amazon and other companies, has succeeded because of the strong, self-perpetuating culture that endures and builds on itself even as thousands of new people pass through in the course of many years. Silbert established and entrenched the culture by embodying its values herself, especially during the early days with those first 50, 100, or 150 people.

Psych Concept #7

Walk the Walk
(Don't Just Talk the Talk)

Howard Gardner, a professor of cognitive science at Harvard and a MacArthur Foundation "genius" award winner, writes in his books *Leading Minds* and *Changing Minds* that leaders persuade us not just by the stories they tell but also by the lives they lead—by personifying the beliefs and ideals they're advocating. In the business world this has long been known as "walking the walk" and not just "talking the talk." It's the simplest of ideas, and yet it's rarely practiced beyond a symbolic gesture here or there. More than anyone I've ever encountered in two decades of reporting on American business, Mimi Silbert really walks the walk—and her example shows the full power of this idea.

Silbert didn't just talk about Delancey being a "family." She lived it:

Family members care for and love one another passionately. Not long after Delancey opened, Silbert divorced her husband and had a decade-long romance with her cofounder John Maher, a former child alcoholic and heroin addict who had spent years in prison for robbery and larceny.

Family members live together. Silbert and Maher resided at Delancey, and Silbert's twin sons, David and Greg, grew up there, hanging out with former pimps and prostitutes. Maher raised his two children there as well.

When some family members are able to make money, they help to support the others. In the early years, before the launch and ultimate success of Delancey's first business, the moving company, Silbert continued to work on the outside as a therapist and consultant, and she put every dollar she earned into Delancey.

"To get the culture started, you have to believe in it, live it, show it, be part of it," Silbert says. "You have to be willing to jump in a hole with people. The leader has to be willing to do it *with* people. 'Change' was a verb and it should stay a verb. It has to happen in *action.* You have to *do it.* I don't think a leader can accomplish major change without being willing to slice yourself open and become part of the change. I say, 'You guys force me to be my best self because I live in a glass house.' "

The leadership of Maher, a former criminal and addict, was crucial to creating the Delancey culture. Maher became a local celebrity in the Bay Area, and his brother graduated from Delancey and was elected to San Francisco's Board of Supervisors, which runs the city along with the mayor. But when Maher began drinking again, he got into a car accident on the Bay Bridge in 1985 while intoxicated, and Delancey forced him to quit. Its rule against alcohol and drugs had to apply to everyone, even the founder. Maher, who had a history of heart disease, died three years later at age forty-eight.

As of 2005 Delancey had more than fourteen thousand "graduates," and while a small percentage eventually return to old addictions or wind up back in prison, overwhelmingly these ex-cons remain lawful, sober, and self-reliant. Deborah graduated in three and a half years and became a sales manager for a nationally known brand. Christina became a manager at a construction company in Sacramento. Gerald became the maître d' at the Delancey Street Restaurant, an experience that would easily qualify him to hold the same position at any number of other restaurants in San Francisco.

In most parts of the nation, companies won't consider employing ex-felons and public housing won't take them. Former convicts return to crime and drugs partly because those are their only options in a culture that demonizes them. But Delancey's local reputation has made it easier for its graduates to find work in northern California. "I teach our people that their goal is to change peoples' perceptions through good human interaction," Silbert says. "At the restaurant with customers, you've shown them that change is possible."

Silbert and the Delancey residents have successfully lobbied to change a number of California state laws that curtailed the freedoms of former felons. They've gotten ex-cons the right to vote. Delancey residents run a polling place at the residential complex. They've gotten the right to be elected to school boards, the right to be licensed as real-estate brokers, the right to be admitted to the bar as attorneys, and the right to hold wine and liquor licenses, and what's even more impressive is that Delancey's graduates have done all of those things. If you've run a multimillion dollar company for Delancey Street, you want and expect opportunities when you re-emerge into the greater society.

In recent years Delancey has expanded, replicating the program in Santa Monica, New York City, Santa Fe, and Greensboro, North

Carolina. Slowly Delancey is beginning to change the public's perception of ex-convicts in those localities. Meanwhile, Silbert still lives in San Francisco at the original Delancey, which for the past thirty-five years has been *her* therapy. She preaches "physician, heal thyself," and takes her own medicine. "I get flat," she says. "All of a sudden, I just don't have any feelings, or I start feeling like a victim. Feeling sorry for myself. And I could get in my bed, surround myself with white chocolate truffles, and think of all the ways I've been betrayed. But then I'll run to the dining room, grab a bunch of new guys, and start talking 'as if' I care. And all of a sudden I'm excited again."

BONUS MINI CASE STUDY
The Parole Officer

In 1983 a man named Kyle Stewart started working as a parole and probation officer in the Iowa state prison system. "There never really was training in how to handle criminals," he recalls. "You would go to college, get a degree in psychology, criminology, or sociology, and then it was on-the-job training."

He absorbed the culture of the criminal justice system and its common-sense approach, which could be called the "kick their ass" approach. He had around one hundred ex-convicts who reported to him, and he told them what to do. He forced them to submit to his authority, which might mean ordering them to take part in a program for substance abuse. The parole officer's relationship with an ex-con is similar to a doctor's relationship with a patient: The expert has the power, quickly makes the diagnosis, and prescribes the cure.

The ex-cons weren't "free" yet—they were supposed to follow Stewart's orders or risk violating their parole—but still, they defended their freedom and self-respect. They didn't want anyone to tell them what to do. And their only ways to preserve self-respect were by arguing and disobeying. So the meetings between parolee and parole officer became confrontational. "If a guy came in and showed any form of 'resistance,' I'd get into a yelling match and kick him out of my office," Stewart says. Often Stewart had to revoke clients' parole and send them back to jail. But the fear of prison didn't get them to change their behavior, overcome their problems, and live as lawful citizens. "Punitive measures have never worked," Stewart says.

While Stewart was kicking their asses, the stress was kicking his own ass. He ended his days frustrated and took Nexium to relieve his heartburn.

Then, a few years ago, the Iowa prison system started sending around some materials about a different approach. It was called "motivational interviewing" and had been developed by psychologists William Miller of the University of New Mexico and Stephen Rollnick of the University of Wales. Stewart was intrigued. "The key is that counselors, physicians, and clinicians see ourselves as the experts with the answers, but we're not listening to the patient," he says. "If they're going to change, they're the ones who are going to do it. We used to dehumanize them, and we need to humanize them."

If Stewart quickly looked over the files on a particular ex-con and saw that the offender was a longtime alcoholic and methamphetamine addict, for example, Stewart might order him to attend a twelve-step program for substance abusers. The offender would "jump through the hoops," Stewart says. "But did I ask him *why* he's a substance abuser? Maybe he's a hundred thousand dollars in debt from gambling and that leads to his drinking and drugs. The bottom line is a financial problem, and I missed the bottom line entirely.

"Then I might say, 'Have you ever thought of Gamblers Anonymous?' The client says: 'It's old senior citizens. It's a bunch of b.s.' I'll say: 'What is it you would like that would help and support you with your gambling problem?' And he'll come up with the answers. He'll start walking the walk. We all have the answers to our problems—it's that we don't dig down to get there. I believe that you can let the client drive."

If the real reason why people don't change is demoralization—the overwhelming sense of hopelessness and powerlessness—then the most basic thing that a parole officer can do is to inspire a new sense of hope and power. By listening and showing respect for the client's opinion, Stewart becomes a source of hope. He inspires their belief that it's possible for them to solve their problems (Key #1). He can encourage them to try new approaches, which might help them learn new skills and new ways of thinking (Key #2 and Key #3). They're more likely to try new things, and persist in the effort, if they're the ones who come up with the plan.

What about the clients who are extremely "resistant" and argumentative? Stewart asks them to think of a scale from one to ten, where ten represents finally getting off probation. "I'll say, 'Tell me how we can get from one to two,' and they'll come up with the answer."

Dean Ornish likes to say, "People don't resist change; they resist being changed," and that's exactly what Stewart has found with his new philosophy. The authoritarianism of parole officers—and, for that matter, nearly everyone in the criminal justice system—encourages "resistance."

"From the minute they're arrested to the minute they're sentenced, everyone is telling them what to do and no one is listening," Stewart says. "You want them to buy in and join up. I don't have to assert my power and authority. They already know that I have the power and authority. We use the phrase: 'I'd rather dance with you than fight with you.' Like a horse whisperer, it's more collaborative rather than trying to break them violently. They know I have the power, but I'm here to work with them."

Stewart and one of his colleagues decided to take their toughest, most argumentative clients and put them together in a weekly conversational group. They invited fourteen ex-convicts representing a variety of racial and ethnic backgrounds and crimes, including sexual offenses, drug dealing, burglary, and drunk driving. None had shown any interest in changing. Stewart spent the ninety-minute session listening to them rather than telling them what to do. "Clients say, 'This is weird and different, not like the hundred other frickin' programs we've been to,' " Stewart says. "In one and a half hours they calmed down. They said 'These guys aren't against us.' Now they come back every week and say, 'At least I'm listened to.'

"In the last year the difference has been *huge*. They want somebody to listen. They put down their guard. They *want* to make a change. Now I don't have to file violations as much. It's unbelievably better. I'm not taking Nexium anymore. I'm not coming home feeling frustrated and beaten up."

CHANGE 101

Cheat Sheet #2

(Crib notes on the theory so far)

CASE STUDY: CRIMINALS

CONVENTIONAL STRATEGY OF THE THREE Fs:
FACTS, FEAR, AND FORCE

Society tries to deter people from lives of crime and drugs with the threat of long, punitive prison sentences. Upon release, parole officers assert strict authority over them.

Why This Fails

FRAMES: People who think with a "criminal mind" instilled by three generations of crime, addiction, and poverty, have no real understanding of the sober, law-abiding life.

REPEAT: Criminals lack the basic habits and skills they need to assimilate into middle-class culture—from the ways to walk and talk to the educational and vocational training.

COMMUNITY: Criminals think, feel, and act in ways that help them survive in the violent cultures of the underclass and prison.

THE CHANGE STRATEGY OF THE THREE Rs

KEY #1 (RELATE): A new relationship with veteran Delancey residents provides new arrivals with hope. They look to the veterans as role models for change. Delancey also gives them an entirely new relationship with their peers, forcing them to learn to become responsible for and accountable to other people.

Psych Concept: Short-term wins. After several months of living without threats, violence, drugs, or alcohol, the new residents realize, to their surprise, that they are indeed capable of being sober and peaceful.

Psych Concept: Walk the walk. Cofounder Mimi Silbert, who has lived for thirty-five years among the four hundred addicted ex-convicts, personifies the program's values and ideals.

KEY #2 (REPEAT): They receive daily training so they can change their "outsides"—how to dress, walk, and talk like members of the middle-class—and practice sobriety and non-violence.

KEY #3 (REFRAME): They learn an entirely new view of the world—the "middle-class mind" instead of the "criminal mind."

Psych Concept: Recasting a life's story. Through the ritual of "Dissipation" and by learning the idea of "balancing the scales," the ex-convicts find a way to deal with the guilt they come to feel about their earlier lives and to see their lives in a different way.

PSYCH CONCEPTS (SO FAR)

1. Frames
2. Denial and other psychological self-defenses
3. Short-term wins
4. The power of community and culture
5. Acting as if
6. Recasting a life's story
7. Walk the walk

CASE STUDY:
Workers

In this chapter I'm going to take a closer look at the transformation of the rebellious workers at the General Motors auto plant in Fremont, California, after it was taken over and run by Toyota in the 1980s. But we need some important context to understand this case study, so I'm going to take you first to Cambridge, Massachusetts, in the 1930s.

This story begins when a young man named Douglas Mac-Gregor was starting out as a professor at Harvard. He asked one of his more experienced colleagues to watch him teach and offer some advice. The older professor told him to stop jingling the coins and keys in his pockets, stop putting his feet up on the desk, and get "a theoretical framework into which to put things."

MacGregor never broke the habit of kicking up his heels. But by the late 1950s he finally came up with a new way of thinking. It was revolutionary back then, and even today, half a century later, it's still astonishing.

He started with an obvious fact: The way that large companies were organized and run was modeled on the Catholic Church and the military, which are hierarchical systems where everyone has a title and a rank. The power and authority flow from the top down through many layers. In the church, God is at the pinnacle, and God speaks through the Pope, who presides over the bishops, and so on down to the parish priests and the great masses of laypeople. In the military the monarch or ruler issues orders to the generals, who command the lieutenants, and so on down to the lowliest soldiers. Because there are many more people at the bottom levels, the structures are thought of as pyramids. The lines of authority are clear: Every person takes orders from only one boss. Communication flows along those lines too: You don't go above your boss's head and try to talk to his or her boss, and your boss doesn't undermine your authority by talking directly to your subordinates. It is all very rigid and clear, and it all depends on everyone following the orders that come down from above.

But *why* do people submit to authority and do what they are told? If they don't, the organizations can punish them severely. For example, when civilians were conscripted into military service, many of them didn't want to put their lives at risk on the battlefield to kill others. But they fought and killed because they had no choice. If they didn't follow orders they could be court-martialed and, in many cases, sentenced to death. Similarly, Catholics who defied the church could be excommunicated, a fate worse than death since they believe it means eternal damnation.

Companies have never had that kind of power, but during the heyday of the industrial revolution, they could be fearsome. William Henry Frick, who ran Andrew Carnegie's steel factories, sent a private militia to shoot at striking workers, and the survivors of the massacre were blacklisted by the industry. When workers were fired, they often had no way to support their families, since public relief was meager and unemployment insurance didn't exist yet.

Even Henry Ford, hailed as the worker's hero, became utterly oppressive. When Ford invented the assembly line, he believed that laborers needed greater incentives to get them to put up with the numbing repetitiveness of the new way of working—which Ford himself called "terrifying." So he astonished the nation by paying wages of five dollars a day, double the standard rate for autoworkers. Eventually, though, Ford came to rely on fear, intimidation, and violence rather than rewards. His foreman yelled at the underlings to work faster and forbade them from talking on the assembly line or taking breaks to go to the bathroom. The laborers were allowed only fifteen minutes for lunch, which forced them to eat so quickly they risked choking. Ford deployed a small army of three thousand armed thugs, street fighters, and mobsters who spied on, blackmailed, and threatened his workers and stifled dissent and union organizing. On one especially infamous occasion, Ford's hoodlums viciously beat up a group of union leaders who were peacefully handing out leaflets outside the gates of the factory.

By the 1950s American workers had formed strong unions and achieved many legal protections. Companies lost much of their power to punish. People still needed their jobs, of course, but in many industries it became much more difficult for bosses to fire them or to force them to work longer or harder.

When MacGregor was teaching at the business school of the Massachusetts Institute of Technology in the late fifties, he realized there could be a much better way to run companies, but it required a new mindset. Corporate executives clung to the old approach—the military model of fear and force, power and authority, command and control, bosses and subordinates—because they had a specific belief system about human nature. In his 1960 book, *The Human Side of Enterprise*, MacGregor called the belief system "Theory X."

According to Theory X, most people naturally disliked work and would avoid it if they could, so they had to be "coerced, controlled, directed" and "threatened with punishment" to get them to work hard enough. "This dislike of work is so strong that even the promise of rewards is not generally enough to overcome it," he wrote. "People will accept the rewards and demand continually higher ones, but these alone will not produce the necessary effort. Only the threat of punishment will do the trick." What's more, the corporate chiefs believed that workers wanted it this way: "The average human being prefers to be directed, wishes to avoid responsibility, has relatively little ambition, wants security above all."

Theory X had prevailed for a long time. But MacGregor was influenced by newer ideas about what motivated people. In the 1940s psychologist Abraham Maslow wrote about "the hierarchy of needs," a notion that has been a staple of Psych 101 courses in colleges ever since. People first have to worry about what they need for survival and security—food, shelter, sleep, money, and safety. But once they satisfy those basic needs, they're motivated by the need for love, affection, belonging, status, recognition, self-esteem, knowledge, creativity, and achievement.

Influenced by Maslow's writings, MacGregor realized that Theory X had it all wrong. People didn't want "security above all." Once they had steady paychecks and union cards that made their jobs secure, they wanted much more. MacGregor exclaimed, "A satisfied need is not a motivator of behavior!" But people couldn't strive for higher needs while working on assembly lines performing narrow tasks that were mindless, repetitive, unvaried, and boring. They had to wait until they left work to engage in other pursuits— such as spending time with their spouses, children, and friends, or enjoying sports and hobbies, or taking part in church and community groups—that made them feel loved, admired, and respected, and gave them a true sense of belonging, and provided them with better outlets for their intelligence and creativity. Even though they liked the money they were paid, they couldn't spend it until they left work. "It is not surprising, therefore, that for many wage earners, *work is perceived as a form of punishment,*" MacGregor wrote.

He believed that work didn't have to be viewed so negatively. MacGregor formulated what he called Theory Y. According to Theory Y, work could be "as natural as play." Most people didn't necessarily dislike work—depending on the situation, work could feel satisfying rather than punishing. And workers didn't have to be controlled or threatened. Instead, they would be motivated when they felt a real sense of belonging and common purpose with their colleagues and when the company gave them opportunities to further their knowledge and be admired and respected for their abilities.

Psych Concept, Revisited

The Power of Community and Culture

In the lingo of *Change or Die,* Maslow's influential theory helped to call attention to the overwhelming importance

> of community in motivating how people think, feel,
> and act.

MacGregor earnestly believed that most individuals could learn not only to accept responsibility, but also to seek it. Many people throughout the organization could be highly imaginative, ingenious, and creative in solving problems at work, not just a few higher-ups. But companies didn't take advantage of the intellectual potential of their people.

MacGregor called Theory Y "an invitation to innovation." But even he believed there were limits to how much change was possible for American business. When a "militant and hostile union" controlled a large factory, he explained, the problems appeared to be "insurmountable."

•

In the early 1980s, General Motors' factories were a flagrant example of the failure of Theory X. Brian Haun, a production supervisor on GM's assembly line in Van Nuys, California, described the situation for hourly wage earners: "In the plant, you're treated like a no-mind idiot," he said. "You're supposed to come in and just put the parts on the car and shut up and do your job, and if you miss one, I'm going to yell at you, and eventually you get so used to the yelling that it doesn't do any good. If you're a supervisor, what can you do? You can't fire them—the union won't let you." Maryann Keller wrote: "Workers were held accountable through a system of intimidation. Do your job and your supervisor won't yell at you. That was a pretty thin incentive!"

One of the bitterest of the many battles between the United

Auto Workers and GM's management was over the company's push to save money by speeding up the production line. "If you passed out, they dragged your body on and kept the line moving," said Diane Cordero, who put together the steel frames of cars at the Fremont plant. "At GM, controlling the assembly line's speed was a fundamental privilege of management," wrote Paul Ingrassia and Joseph B. White, who won a Pulitzer Prize for their coverage of the auto business in the *Wall Street Journal*. "Old-line GM plant managers would sooner pass out hand grenades at the plant gate than allow a laborer to slow down the line."

GM's chiefs were typical of America's captains of industry in their belief that they had to control, coerce, and threaten their underlings. Theory X ruled the business world. "American companies tend, fundamentally, to mistrust workers, whether they are salaried employees or blue-collar workers," Keller wrote. "There is a pervading attitude that 'if you give them an inch, they'll take a mile,' because they really don't want to work. The idea, for example, that a worker in the plant would have the power to stop the line in order to eliminate a problem was heresy. Would such permission lead to widespread line-stoppage for every whim?"

At GM's Fremont plant, the workers and the managers battled over seemingly everything. In 1982 the local union was fighting more than six hundred unresolved grievances, including more than sixty contested firings. When GM shuttered the plant, the company gave only two weeks' notice to the workers, which made them even more embittered.

Toyota decided to revive the operation, but its executives didn't want to take back the unruly workers. *Fortune* described the Fremont employees as "a tough Bay Area crew: blacks from the Oakland ghetto, Chicanos from the barrios of San Jose, rednecks from the local bars, and the inevitable handful of leftist militants out of the Berkeley street scene." Toyota hired former U.S. secretary of labor William Usery as its consultant for labor relations in America, and he told a reporter: "Commies and drug addicts, gambling, fighting, refusing to work—that was Toyota's idea of a unionized American work force."

When the UAW insisted that Toyota take back the original employees, the Japanese executives acquiesced.

KEY #1
Relate

Once they agreed to take back the former employees, Toyota's managers trusted the union workers and treated them with respect instead of with hostility and fear. GM had called these workers "unmanageable," but Toyota's chiefs assumed the workers instinctively wanted to do a good job.

When the two companies began their partnership, called "Nummi," Toyota sent 450 of the U.S. workers to Toyota City in Japan for three days of on-the-job training at its Takoaka plant. The Americans saw that Toyota trusted its workers to pull cords or push buttons to stop the assembly lines if they saw a defective car or if they were having a problem. Toyota gave responsibility and accountability to its production workers, and the workers responded by acting responsibly and being accountable.

The Americans were getting their first look at life in a Theory Y company. Toyota's "secret" was to treat workers "with respect, encourage them to think independently, allow them to make decisions, and make them feel connected to an important effort," Keller writes in *Rude Awakening*. She explains that Toyota's philosophy was based on two ideas: "The first was that the average worker is motivated by the desire to do a job that enhances his self-worth and earns the respect of other workers. The second premise was that the worker is inspired by an employer who places value in the worker's input."

KEY #2
Repeat

Toyota trains the workers in new habits and skills.

•

When GM was running the Fremont plant, the hourly workers were bound by eighty-two different job classifications. The work rules restricted them to performing the specific tasks of their exact job descriptions and prevented them from helping their coworkers. A pipe fitter couldn't touch a fuse. An electrician wasn't permitted anywhere near a pipe. Assembly workers couldn't lend one another a hand. The workers did their own little jobs and felt disconnected from their colleagues and alienated from any notion of a greater purpose or mission.

When Nummi began, Toyota decided that all assembly workers would have the same job classification. Toyota put them into small teams of eight to ten people led by fellow hourly workers. The team leaders weren't bosses. They were more like coaches or instructors. The teammates were all trained to do one another's job. Often they were also taught to handle the work of other people on other teams nearby on the factory floor. Instead of having to perform the same boring, mindless, repetitive work, they learned as many as fifteen different jobs. The initial team leaders were the 450 people who had trained at Toyota City, but eventually every team member learned to be a leader and took turns. While GM had deployed scores of bosses to threaten and yell at the workers, Nummi trusted the teams to solve most of the problems that arose and to stop the line at their own discretion. "Line workers, who'd never been allowed to make a move without a foreman's approval under GM, now virtually controlled the pace of work," wrote Ingrassia and White in *Comeback: The Fall and Rise of the American Auto Industry*. Nummi also relied on workers to find ways to make the work easier and save money. It turned out the workers were imaginative, ingenious, and creative.

KEY #3

Reframe

Nummi obliterated the barrier that had separated "we" and "they." One of the key points of Toyota's philosophy was "treating every employee as a manager." And that's what happened in Fremont. Once there was only a "we," the workers felt a true sense of belonging. Keller writes: "When a worker is accountable to his peers, not to a distant, oppressive supervisor, performance improves, because workers don't want to let the rest of the team down by not showing up for work or doing a shoddy job." One of the Nummi laborers, Santos Martinez, said, "I learned a different meaning for the word respect—one that doesn't include fear. My responsibility is now to the team, which works together like a family to solve problems and do the job. And no one places blame when something goes wrong." Another worker on the factory floor, Lester Meyers, said, "At GM, no one cared what you thought. Here you're included in everything within the unit."

The results were extraordinary. Nummi quickly began producing cars that had hardly any defects, while other GM plants routinely had dozens of defects per car. *Consumer Reports* wrote that the Chevy Novas Nummi turned out were "a class act among small cars" and had been "assembled, fitted, and finished as well as any Toyota we have seen." And the new secretary of labor named Nummi America's best model of labor-management cooperation.

Psych Concepts, Revisited
"Framing" and "Denial"

What's most intriguing about the Nummi story isn't that Theory Y worked. It's that GM's managers didn't learn the lessons of the experiment. They were looking for how Toyota applied its technology, so they missed the real "secret," which was how the Japanese company tapped into the workers' psychology.

In its heyday GM had been extraordinarily dominant in its business. It captured 60 percent of the U.S. car market in 1960, selling twice as many cars as Ford and Chrysler combined and six times as many as all the imported brands. But GM's executives developed a superiority complex, and for decades they remained in denial about their cars' quality problems.

They had the *facts* from the beginning. In 1960 GM's

engineers came up with a one-hundred-point scale for comparing the quality of the cars produced by the company's many factories. A perfect car would score one hundred. Every defect would knock off a point from the total. It turned out that many of GM's plants typically made cars with forty or more defects. They posted scores of sixty or below. That was embarrassing, since everyone remembered their own school days, when a sixty was an F, a failing grade. By the late 1960s, GM's executives found a solution. They didn't improve the quality of the cars—they didn't know how. Besides, their cars weren't any worse than their competition's. Instead, they recalibrated the scale so 145 would represent a perfect score. This way, all of GM's plants would score one hundred or higher. A-plus! When a plant scored 130, employees would throw a celebration even though the cars still averaged fifteen defects. No customer would celebrate buying that car.

Even as the Japanese imports began developing a reputation for high quality with American consumers, GM didn't change. The 145-point system lasted for two decades, through the late eighties. By early 1985, three months after Nummi began making cars, it was averaging 140, nearly perfect. Eventually Nummi reached 145, turning out cars that had no flaws. Still, GM's top executives in Detroit didn't learn from Nummi.

Finally, in 1992, after GM posted an annual loss of $4.5 billion, its board of directors got rid of the company's leaders and replaced them with younger reformers. The new chief executive officer, Jack Smith, proclaimed that

GM would transform all its factories to be like Nummi and Toyota.

But the Theory X company never entirely believed in Theory Y. Its bosses remained in denial even as GM faced possible bankruptcy in the first decade of the new century. The facts haven't set them free. They still believe what they want to believe. "Even in the face of vast research to the contrary, Detroit for years has convinced itself of the notion, completely unsubstantiated, that its vehicles are every bit as good as those built by the import companies," wrote *New York Times* reporter Micheline Maynard in *The End of Detroit.* "In fact, this was the very claim made one morning in November 2002 by General Motors vice chairman Bob Lutz when he declared GM's vehicles the equal of those built by Honda and Toyota. Yet that afternoon, GM recalled 1.5 million minivans." In the first three months of 2004, GM had to spend $200 million recalling 7.5 million vehicles, including some of its newest and most popular models.

BONUS MINI CASE STUDY
Gore-Tex Reframes the Corporation

In the late 1950s one of Douglas MacGregor's speeches about Theory Y had a strong influence on a man named Wilbert L. Gore, who went by "Bill." Gore was an unlikely revolutionary. Forty-five years old, he was a somewhat nerdy, quiet, humble man who lived in a small house in Newark, Delaware. He had worked for seventeen years as a chemical engineer at DuPont, but he was frustrated by the "authoritarian" nature of large companies, which he felt smothered creativity. He realized that the car pool was the only place where people talked to one another freely without regard for the chain of command. He also observed that when there was a crisis, the company created a task force and threw out the rules. It was the only time when organizations took risks and made actual breakthroughs. Why, he wondered, should you have to wait for a crisis? Why not just throw out the rules anyway? And why not do away with hierarchy and ranks and titles while you're at it? Why not create an organization where everyone could speak freely with anyone else?

Bill and his wife, Genevieve, who was known as "Vieve," decided to start their own company. Many of their friends thought they were foolish. They had five children to support, including two who were in college, and Bill was up for a big promotion at DuPont. But they were motivated by creativity and achievement, not by security. On January 1, 1958—their twenty-third wedding anniversary—they had dinner at home, and then Vieve said, "Well, let's clear up the dishes and get to work." And that's how W. L. Gore & Associates was founded. They mortgaged their house, withdrew four thousand dollars out of their savings, and raised extra capital from their bridge club. Their first few coworkers lived in their basement, accepting room and board instead of salaries. It's a classic story of an entrepreneurial venture in every way except one: Even as W. L. Gore grew tremendously over the years, and even as it created one of the best-known brand names in America—"Gore-Tex," a plastic coating that makes clothing waterproof and windproof—and even as it hired thousands of new workers and earned billions of dollars in annual sales, the company still had *no bosses*.

Bill Gore organized the company as though it were a bunch of car pools or task forces. He made sure each of the manufacturing plants and office buildings had 150 people at most, which kept things small enough so that everyone could get to know one another, learn what everyone else was working on, and discover who had the skills and knowledge to get something accomplished, whether they were trying to solve a problem or create a new product.

When I tell people that W. L. Gore has no bosses, they usually don't believe me, because the fact doesn't fit into their frames. Our thinking is still dominated by Theory X and the idea that large companies can operate only on the military command-and-control model. When people go to work at Gore, they're *told* how the place works, but it takes them a long time to grasp the reality.

That's what happened to Diane Davidson. Nothing in her fifteen years of experience as a sales executive in the apparel industry prepared her for life in a company where there are no bosses or pyramids.

"When I arrived at Gore, I didn't know who did what," she said. "I wondered how anything got done here. It was driving me crazy." Like all new hires, Davidson was brought into the company by a "sponsor" who would serve as her mentor, not as her boss. The sponsor would be there whenever she asked for advice but would never evaluate her performance or make decisions about her pay or give her assignments or orders. But she simply didn't know *how* to work without someone telling her what to do.

"Who's my boss?" she kept asking.

"Stop using the B-word," her sponsor replied.

As an experienced executive, Davidson assumed that Gore's talk was typical corporate euphemism rather than actual practice.

"Secretly, there are bosses, right?" she asked.

There weren't. She eventually figured it out: "Your team is your boss, because you don't want to let them down. Everyone's your boss, and no one's your boss."

What's more, Davidson saw that people didn't fit into standardized job descriptions. They had all made different sets of "commitments" to their teams, often combining roles that remained segregated in different fiefdoms at conventional companies, such as sales, marketing, and product design. It took months for Davidson to get to know all her teammates and what they did—and for them to get to know her and offer her responsibilities. The "associates" at Gore all get to decide for themselves what new commitments they want to take on. Individuals could design their roles to fit their own interests and strengths. Everyone is supposed to be like an "amoeba" and take on a unique shape. They aren't forced into preconceived boxes or standardized niches. At the end of the year a committee forms and reviews each associate's contribution and decides on salaries and bonuses, the same way it works at law firms.

Davidson's experience is typical at Gore. "You join a team and you're an idiot," says John Morgan, who has switched into new teams five times throughout a twenty-year tenure. "It takes eighteen months to build credibility. Early on, it's really frustrating. In hindsight, it makes sense. As a sponsor, I tell new hires, 'Your job for the first six months is to get to know the team,' but they have trouble believing it."

Gore is the only major American company that has put Theory Y into full effect, and its results have been extraordinary. When *Fortune* publishes its rankings of the "best places to work in America,"

Gore is always at the top of the list or very close to it. And *Fast Company* wrote that Gore is "pound for pound, the most innovative company in America." A few years ago the Gore people realized that their company made twice as much profit per employee as DuPont. Even though Gore hires many new associates directly out of college, it has recruited thousands of people from Theory X companies. It takes newcomers a while to get used to things, but being immersed in a Theory Y culture changes how they think, feel, and act. That's the power of community.

CHANGE 101

Cheat Sheet #3
(Crib notes on the theory so far)

CASE STUDY: WORKERS

THE CONVENTIONAL STRATEGY OF THE THREE Fs:
FACTS, FEAR, AND FORCE

Plant foremen sped up the production line and yelled at workers to try to force them to work faster, and the company threatened to replace the workers with robots.

Why This Fails

The adversarial relationship between labor and management motivated workers to fight back against their bosses.

THE CHANGE STRATEGY OF THE THREE Rs

KEY #1 (RELATE): Toyota created a new relationship with workers by putting them into small teams led by fellow workers. Toyota also inspired a new sense of hope by taking the team leaders to Japan to show them that this system was actually in effect there and worked extremely well.

Psych Concept: The Power of Community. Workers became strongly motivated because of their new sense of responsibility and accountability to their peers.

KEY #2 (REPEAT): Toyota taught workers the new skills and jobs they needed to succeed in the Theory Y approach to manufacturing and gave them the opportunity to practice and perfect this new kind of teamwork on the assembly line.

KEY #3 (REFRAME): When workers saw that Toyota was actually treating them like members of a family—by giving them respect, responsibility, and a sense of accountability—they began to think of themselves as part of a large family.

PSYCH CONCEPTS (SO FAR)

1. Frames
2. Denial and other psychological self-defenses
3. Short-term wins
4. The power of community and culture
5. Acting as if
6. Recasting a life's story
7. Walk the walk

PART TWO

Change 102

APPLYING THE THREE KEYS

Changing Your Life, Your Company, Your Industry, and More . . .

Changing Your Own Life

The first part of this book showed that even in the most seemingly "impossible" situations, profound change *is* possible. Forget about using the excuse that "people don't change" or its natural follow-up, "I can't change."

Still, we all know from experience that change can be daunting. In this chapter I'll look at new science that explains why this is so, and then I'm going to talk about how individuals can apply the three keys to bringing about change in their own lives.

Change doesn't have to be something that happens to you. You can make it happen—actively, intentionally, and deliberately—if you develop an understanding of how change really works. Let's look at insights from neuroscience about what frustrates change and how to make it easier.

Psych Concept #8

The Brain Is Plastic

As I'm writing this book in 2006, General Motors is struggling to avoid bankruptcy, a great symbol of failure. But
GM's real problem, at the root of it all, was *success*. As
we've already seen, the company once controlled 60 percent of the U.S. auto market, selling more than twice as
many cars and trucks as Ford and Chrysler and six times
as many as all the imports combined. GM was so successful for so long that its culture and people became
set in their ways. When the auto industry began changing
dramatically, it didn't. When I talked with one of the
world's leading neuroscientists, I found that the problem
of repeated success and expertise honed over a long
period of time faces all of us as individuals.

Here's an example: If you were born and grew up in
the United States, you've surely been very successful for
a long time—since early childhood, actually—at understanding and speaking English. Today, if you tried your
hardest to learn French, say, or Chinese, or Swahili, you'd
constantly struggle, and make mistakes, and feel like an
idiot. And who wants to feel like an idiot?

Scientists used to believe that our brains became
"hardwired" early in life—the circuitry is finished and
can't be rewired. Then researchers began performing
"brain scans" using functional Magnetic Resonance Im-
agery (fMRI) machines, which produced vividly detailed
pictures that enabled them to actually see how particular

sections of the brain had expanded or contracted over time. They realized that the brain's ability to change—its so-called *plasticity*—is lifelong. We *can* learn complex new things in our thirties or even our eighties. So why don't we?

That's the question I discussed with Michael Merzenich, a professor of neuroscience at the University of California at San Francisco. "Merz," as he's fondly known, was a pioneer in the study of brain plasticity and remains one of its leading figures. He's relaxed, affable, and fat. As he munches on potato chips, I wonder whether he's heard about the programs run by his colleague at UCSF, Dr. Dean Ornish. Merz's intelligence is so inspiring that I keep worrying his heart won't last long enough for the world to get the fullest possible benefit of his brain.

Merzenich begins to explain his field by talking about rats. You can train a rat to have a new skill. The rat solves a puzzle, and you give it a food reward. After two hundred times, it can remember how to solve the puzzle for nearly its lifetime. The rat has developed a habit. It can perform the task automatically because its brain has changed.

Similarly, people have thousands of habits—such as how to use a pen—that we perform automatically because we've created lasting changes in our brains through repetition. For highly trained specialists, such as professional musicians, the changes show up conspicuously on brain scans. If you've practiced an instrument several hours a day for a couple of decades, it makes a big difference. Flute players, for instance, have especially large physical representations in their brains in the areas that control the fingers, tongue, and lips. "They've distorted their brains," Merzenich explains.

Businesspeople are also highly trained specialists and they've distorted their brains as well. An older executive "has powers that a younger person walking in the door doesn't have," Merzenich says. He has a great number of specialized skills and abilities. A specialist is a difficult thing to create and is valuable for a corporation but specialization also instills an inherent "rigidity." The cumulative weight of experience makes it more difficult to change.

How can people overcome these factors? Merzenich says the key is keeping up the brain's machinery for learning. "When you're young, almost everything you do is behavior-based learning—it's an incredibly powerful, plastic period," he says. "What happens that becomes stultifying is you stop learning and you stop using the machinery, so it starts dying." Unless you work on it, brain fitness begins declining at around age thirty for men and a little later for women. "People mistake 'being active' for continuous learning," Merzenich says. "The machinery is only activated by learning. People think they're leading an interesting life when they haven't learned anything in twenty or thirty years." Comfortable with our successes, we're reluctant to be like Merz's lab rat and struggle with a new puzzle hundreds of times until we can solve it effortlessly. We're averse to the arduous practice and relentless repetition that drives changes in our brains.

If you're the senior tax partner at a large corporate law firm, then reading the latest journal articles about the tax code isn't what Merz means by "learning." The law partner is already an expert at that kind of precise verbal reasoning. In that case, real learning might mean taking beginner's lessons in downhill skiing or ballroom dancing. The idea is to escape from your expertise and become a novice in an entirely different pursuit. It's about taking on challenges that you'll be bad at for quite a while rather than always returning to pursuits you've been good at for many years. And it's about using different kinds of intelligence—verbal, mechanical, physical, mathematical, and such. That's why learning a foreign language or a musical instrument is a particularly valuable exercise for brain fitness. "My suggestion is learn Spanish or the oboe," Merz says.

You'll know that you're learning something truly new and different if it's really hard for a long time and you're constantly making mistakes and struggling and feeling like an idiot until you get better at it and the habits and skills become automatic. Complex new learning is difficult and discouraging. Think of trying for the first time to drive a stick shift, play golf, or dance the tango. That's why it's so helpful to have a good teacher or coach. The best teachers do much more than demonstrate technique and correct errors. They inspire and sustain hope by communicating their belief in you and pointing out the small improvements you're making, which often you don't notice yourself. They *sell* you on their competence, they sell you on their methods, and most important, they sell you on your own potential.

Change of *every kind* is about learning new habits and skills (Key #2) that inform new ways of thinking (Key #3). Change is all about training and teaching, but it takes a lot of "selling" (Key #1) to motivate people to sustain the necessary effort over time.

Once you've reframed the idea of change in this way, then another aspect of the process becomes clearer. When you're learning to play a sport, play a musical instrument, or speak a foreign language, it's not enough to have a skillful teacher who practices a valid method of teaching; it's best to have the *right* teacher for you. The first key to change is about establishing new relationships, and that's inherently tricky because it involves matching up personalities. There must be a real sense of connection and chemistry. There must be a good "fit" between the student and the teacher.

Think of dating and marriage as an example of the odds of forming very close personal relationships. People usually go on plenty of bad dates and have a number of attempts at relationships before ultimately meeting someone who will become an enduring and important part of their lives and change their feelings and thoughts. The same is often true when you try to find what you might call a "change agent"—a mentor, teacher, trainer, coach, or role model.

I found this out the hard way through firsthand experience during two memorable times when I struggled for years with learning and change.

The first ordeal was my frustration and repeated failure when I tried to learn French. When I attended Princeton University in the eighties, the requirements for graduation included passing three semesters of college courses in a foreign language. The only way to get out of this requirement was to score seven hundred or higher out of a possible eight hundred on the College Board Achievement Test. I had gotten A's during four years of high-school French, and I scored 690 on the exam, a very good score, which meant that I could skip ahead and start in the third and final semester-long course that Princeton required. So I enrolled in French 108, feeling self-assured and optimistic—after all, I had nearly "tested out"— only to find myself in a humiliating situation.

Only French was spoken in the class, which was so small there was nowhere to hide. My ability to listen to and speak French was awful. The French teacher at my public high school had conducted the class in English, and the class sizes there were simply too large for any individual pupil to get much of a chance to practice speaking in front of a group. So I still had a lot to learn. I spoke haltingly. My accent was comically bad.

I was extremely self-conscious about looking foolish and incompetent among my new classmates. Princeton was a small college where nearly all the students lived very close together on a campus bordered by a lake, open fields, and a little upscale town that didn't cater much to them. The school was a self-contained community, a tightly knit social realm, where word of mouth spread quickly, and I didn't want to develop a lasting reputation as a blundering idiot. I was so overwhelmed by fear when called upon in French class that I would experience a weird temporary amnesia and momentarily forget nearly all of the grammar and vocabulary that I had learned in high school, the hard-gained knowledge that had enabled me to score so well on the College Board test.

I dreaded attending French 108, which met every weekday

morning and inevitably made me depressed for the rest of the day. I hated feeling so inferior to my classmates, many of whom had attended expensive private schools, such as St. Paul's or Exeter, where French was spoken in the classroom and they became comfortable and adept at it. What's more, they typically came from wealthier families and had spent long vacations or even entire summers living in France while I had never traveled anywhere abroad. I hated the notion that they would look down on my incompetence and utter lack of sophistication.

During the first few weeks of the semester, before the midterm exam, Princeton allowed students to "drop" a course—withdrawing without any penalties or consequences, not even a record on your transcript that you had ever enrolled in it. So that's what I did during the fall of my freshman year. Every term I would return to campus, enroll in French 108, endure two or three weeks of public humiliation, and then drop the course all over again. I did this as a sophomore, a junior, and even as a senior, which raised the question of how I'd qualify for a diploma. I had fulfilled every other requirement for graduation, but I couldn't bring myself to suffer through a full semester of French.

So I decided that I would cram for the College Board's French test, score a seven hundred, and fulfill the requirement that way instead. My roommates and other close friends tried to tell me that I was deceiving myself: Few Princeton students had scored seven hundred or higher on the College Board's *English* tests even though they were native English speakers and were among the best students in America to boot. It was beyond foolish of me to expect that I could pass the French version by locking myself away with a bunch of textbooks.

I took the exam and once again scored in the high six hundreds. Not good enough.

I went to the dean's office and pleaded and cajoled for a small act of mercy, but the university wouldn't compromise its high standards. They weren't going to bend the rules out of sympathy for me.

It looked as though I was going to be a college dropout, an idea that was profoundly disappointing and probably even shameful to my parents, especially since they had saved and sacrificed to enable me to attend such an expensive private university. My father (a PhD engineering professor) and my mother (a schoolteacher) were both the first in their families to go to college. They had attended city-run public institutions where the tuition was free; they had both lived at home and commuted to school by bus or subway. It meant so much to them that their son would graduate from a world-renowned university, but I was blowing it all because I couldn't master a single subject. Although this certainly wasn't a case of "change or die," my demoralization could have real and lasting consequences.

I was nearly resigned to the idea of never graduating, but somehow I mustered the courage to take another French class—this time, a noncredit "adult education" night course at New York University. It turned out that this was a much better place for me to learn. Since I wasn't living in a tight-knit community with my classmates, I felt far less self-conscious around them. I didn't mind looking like an idiot among people whom I would never have to see outside of the classroom. Their opinions wouldn't affect my standing in any of my social circles. So I participated fully in class and made the kinds of mistakes you have to make before you finally improve.

It also helped that I liked my new teacher, an NYU staffer named Professor Gilon. Before long I hired him for frequent one-on-one private tutoring sessions. I loved how he treated me: *not* like a pitiful, struggling dunce of a student (which is what I was in spoken French) but as an intelligent person who was capable of tackling and triumphing over difficult challenges (which is what I was like in every other subject). And I loved that he was an articulate New York intellectual with a great sense of humor who lived in an apartment on the border of Greenwich Village and SoHo and had a passionate interest in the arts and culture—which was *exactly* what I aspired to become. He treated me as a true peer, and most of our lessons were spent in long conversations (in French) about books, music, and film. I wanted to learn from his knowledge about those topics as much as I wanted to learn the mysterious way to properly pronounce a rolling French *r*. I looked forward to our private lessons as fervently as I had loathed French 108. It probably strengthened our bond that we were both Jewish—he would amuse me by sprinkling his French with obscure Yiddish words. I felt he respected me, understood me, and believed in me, and those qualities inspired me to stick out the struggle and practice, learn, and master a skill that had eluded me.

After a few months I returned to Princeton and sat for an oral examination with the chairman of the French department, an intimidating scholar of nineteenth-century French literature. I passed and finally received my degree.

A couple of years later, after I had accumulated some vacation time from working as a reporter on the staff at *Fortune* magazine, I traveled alone to Paris for a full month. I found myself striking up conversations with people seemingly everywhere—cafés, trains,

Laundromats—and quickly developing friendships and being invited to their homes for dinner. The French were fascinated with me because I reminded them of a young Woody Allen—a somewhat neurotic New York Jewish writer who shared a number of their cultural passions and obsessions. They were charmed when I spoke French with remnants of a New York accent that may have dismayed the Princeton faculty. Even though I knew that I was constantly making errors in grammar and vocabulary, they complimented me on how good my French was compared with the efforts of so many Americans. Their interest, acceptance, and support made me even less self-conscious, so I became more adventurous in conversation. I have no doubt that my French improved more in four weeks in France than four years of high school, which is surely a common experience among many students.

Looking back, the lessons of those years are obvious to me: It wasn't that I was incapable of learning French (although that's what I nearly came to believe). It was that I needed new relationships with the right person (Professor Gilon) and the right communities (NYU adult education class and Parisian friends instead of preppy, snobby French 108 students). Most of my Princeton classmates had no problem learning foreign languages from their teachers and with their fellow Princetonians, but I needed different relationships. Learning and change aren't one-size-fits-all phenomena.

At the time, though, I didn't glean the lessons about change from that episode. Then I encountered an even more serious problem that lasted for such a long time that I nearly gave up hope I could ever overcome it.

I can't remember exactly when I became obese. It sounds ridiculous to say that obesity snuck up on me, or that I wasn't really aware that it was happening at the time. I have to search through old photos to try to pin down the range of dates when it must have happened. I do know for sure that I was still slender at twenty-five. It's proven by a photo of me that appeared next to the editor's letter in *Fortune* in the summer of 1990. I had written a cover story titled "The 25 Year Olds," reporting on what my generation thought about their lives and careers. Was that the last picture that captured my thinness? I couldn't have been carrying more than 155 or 160 pounds on my not-quite five-foot-nine frame—the same healthy weight of my college years.

Two years later, when I moved from New York City to San Francisco to become the magazine's West Coast correspondent, I acquired a California driver's license. After it expired I tossed it into a box with my papers from those years, and it remains as documentary evidence of my passage into obesity. "Weight: two hundred." Surely I lied on the application and my actual weight was several pounds higher. There's no denying that within two years I had gained at least forty pounds, maybe even as many as fifty, and gone from being slender to being blatantly overweight. Then I crossed the line into the "O"-zone.

For nearly a decade I remained obese and became even more so. Although I was able to avoid thinking about it most of the time, there were some inevitable episodes that temporarily broke through the psychological defense of my self-deception. For example, when I left my staff job at age thirty to work for myself, I was no longer covered by the company's health insurance, so I had to buy my own policy. I found out I was so overweight that my application would have been automatically rejected. So I lied on the application and somehow got away with it, probably thanks to the compassion of an agent who ignored what he saw.

At thirty-one, when I moved back to New York to take a job as a senior writer for GQ, I was up to 222 pounds. I know this figure only because it was published in my first article for the monthly men's magazine. GQ's editors recruited the chief "personal trainer" at what was then the hottest chain of upscale gyms in the city—Equinox—to use all of the company's manpower and resources to help me lose weight: its trainers, its dieticians, and even its massage therapists.

I worked out daily with Equinox's highly priced, number one trainer Rich Beretta, whose business card identified him by the bodybuilding title he had won: "Mr. America." What I recall most vividly about him are his calf muscles, which looked like the clusters of steel cables that hold up suspension bridges. Rich was entirely amiable, but I could never see him as a role model. No matter what I did, or how hard I tried, I knew that I would never look anything like him or be like him.

Rich seemed to belong to a different species. So did most of the other customers who worked out at Equinox's Union Square location. The place was filled with beautiful people—the club was rumored to give free memberships to models and actors. The rationale was that their hot bodies would create the kind of ambiance likely to lure bankers and lawyers to pay the club's high fees. I never felt comfortable going to that gym to work out on my own—I was much too self-conscious and felt out of place.

I lost about six pounds in the first six weeks, but before long I gained it all back and put on an additional six pounds, which brought up my weight to its all-time peak of 228. The magazine's editor in chief Art Cooper tried to bribe me to lose weight with the promise of a free Hugo Boss suit if I got down to two hundred pounds. But he also liked to take me out to blowout lunches at famous restaurants, especially the Four Seasons, where we would start with martinis and proceed to steaks and red wine. In the afternoon I would try to nap on my small office sofa, but at 5:00 or 5:15 the sounds of Frank Sinatra or Ella Fitzgerald would begin coming out of Art's office. I would stop by and the two of us would spend another couple of hours sitting and talking while I sipped single malt Scotch from Art's bar instead of going to work out before dinner.

At thirty-three I moved back to San Francisco, rented an apartment in the Noe Valley neighborhood, and joined the Purely Physical Fitness gym, just four short blocks away from where I lived and worked. It was very convenient, but I went there so rarely that I thought of it as Purely Theoretical Fitness. I was nearly resigned to the idea that I was an obese person and I simply wasn't going to change. It was becoming my identity. After all, the top trainer in New York had tried his best and even his heroic efforts hadn't helped me.

One day, prodded by my girlfriend, I walked over to the gym so I could work out, only to find that the treadmills and stair-climbers and racks of barbells were gone. The business had closed down months earlier and I hadn't known because I hadn't been there in all that time. Talk about a humiliating moment.

So I got in my car and drove ten minutes to a nearby neighborhood, Cole Valley, where I joined a small, friendly gym called Cole Valley Fitness. As part of the membership I was entitled to two free sessions with one of the gym's personal trainers—actually, this was more of a requirement than an option, since the idea was partly that the trainer would make sure new members knew the proper ways to use the heavy equipment and didn't hurt themselves on the weight-lifting machines. The other unspoken rationale was that after those two free sessions, a new member might decide to hire the trainer on a regular basis.

That's how I wound up beginning a new relationship with a personal trainer named Claudia Berman, who exuded energy and an infectious enthusiasm for exercise. We quickly developed an easy rapport. After the two free sessions, I hired her to train me twice a week and later upped it to three times a week. I bonded with Claudia partly because of our similar backgrounds and interests and partly because I was intrigued by our differences. We both came from Jewish families that prized intellectual and cultural achievement—her parents were physicians and accomplished musicians. We both had elite educations and creative careers in brutally competitive fields marked by high pressure and unhealthy lifestyles. She had graduated from the San Francisco Conservatory of Music and spent several years singing opera in Italy, where her colleagues ridiculed her interest in exercise and argued that it was bad for the voice. Ultimately she switched careers and became a trainer back in California.

While we worked out together I enjoyed talking with her about classical music—I had a subscription to the San Francisco Opera at the time. Unlike "Mr. America," Claudia wasn't from another planet—she was from my planet, which made a big difference. She was like me in so many ways that it made me believe that I could be like her in the other ways—that maybe I could become fit and vibrantly healthy.

Within months I had lost forty pounds. From 228 pounds, my weight dropped to 188, and it has stayed roughly in that range five years since. I lost six inches from my waist. I went from dreading the idea of running a one-quarter mile lap around the track to looking forward to going out and running three miles on my own.

After my weight loss, many friends asked me questions about the specifics of the training regime—what kind of weight lifting or aerobic exercise did Claudia have me do, or what diet did she advise me to follow. Whether the challenge is losing weight or whether it's any other kind of difficult change, we like to think that the "magic" comes from discovering the right process. But the three keys to change suggest that the most important thing is the people, especially having a relationship with people who believe in you and whom you believe in as well.

One of Claudia's great gifts is that she truly believes and expects that her clients will learn to love exercise, even if they haven't worked out much in their pasts. She once told me that she's had clients who've *never* exercised and it excites her to think that maybe they'll wind up becoming marathon runners. Claudia's sincere, absolute belief in her clients' potential helps to inspire their own beliefs.

Claudia's approach also takes advantage of the psychology of short-term wins. She knows that if she can just get clients to commit to several weeks of sessions, the benefits they'll feel from the workouts will be the best advertisement for sticking with the program. When prospective clients tell her, "I don't like exercise," she often replies: "Let's talk about it while taking a walk."

Unfortunately, it took me nearly a decade to find Claudia, and even then I found her only by accident thanks to a weirdly lucky twist of fate. Change *happened* to me. I didn't *make* change happen. The lesson, going forward, is that the next time I'm stuck with difficult problems I haven't been able to solve through my own efforts, I should actively seek out a new relationship—and be well aware that it may take time and persistence to find the right one.

We often prefer to think that change is all about the right process, but what's more important are the *people*. The reason that I achieved such terrific results from working with Claudia and such disappointment from training with Mr. America isn't that Claudia taught me yoga and had me run up stairs while Mr. America gave me lessons in boxing. It's that I connected with Claudia in an emotional way, and our relationship inspired and sustained my belief and commitment.

Just because Mr. America didn't change my life doesn't mean that personal training doesn't "work" or that it couldn't work for me. It simply meant that he wasn't the right trainer for me. When you realize that change depends on relationships, then you can seek a "change agent" much as you do any other important, emotionally charged relationship with a person or community, whether it's seeking a lover or spouse, or joining a church or spiritual group, or hiring colleagues for your company. It's a hit-or-miss endeavor that takes time, energy, frustration, and resilience. But when you find the right relationship, anything is possible.

•

The first key to change doesn't have to mean forming a new emotional relationship with a new person. It can involve a new relationship with a new community. Indeed, one of the most difficult aspects of profound change is that it often forces you to make a sharp break from the old community that has shaped your beliefs up until then. When you absorb a dramatically new way of thinking, feeling, and acting, you face possible rejection or alienation from the colleagues, friends, and family members who shared your old conceptual frameworks. The way you're living no longer makes sense to them. It seems ridiculous or wrong. It simply doesn't fit with their beliefs, values, assumptions, and expectations. Changing your own life often means changing your community, which is hard to foresee and very difficult to get through.

That's a lesson I learned from one of my neighbors in San Francisco, Tim O'Mahoney, who had given up a career in corporate finance and become a carpenter and cabinetmaker. His remarkable transformation meant more than taking a big decrease in income—what he jokingly refers to as his "vow of poverty." In the minds of his former peers and his closest family members, it meant he was taking a big step down in class, from white to blue collar, and that he was rejecting their values and way of life.

When I asked Tim what had enabled him to change his life in such a dramatic way, he told me his story.

Tim grew up in an upper-middle-class family in suburban neighborhoods: They lived in Upper St. Clair, near Pittsburgh, until he was fifteen years old, and then they moved to Lake Bluff, outside of Chicago. Both were places where adults were highly educated, professional, and successful. "Growing up I was always conscious of what my friends' parents did," Tim recalls. "They were surgeons and corporate attorneys."

The O'Mahoney clan fit in well with this elite culture: Tim's parents and his three older sisters had graduate degrees. His father had a masters in business administration from Indiana University and worked as the vice president of marketing and strategic planning for a sizeable corporation. Tim's siblings—he was the youngest of five children—all went on to professional careers as lawyers, dentists, or business executives.

"I was strongly influenced by our parents and our surroundings," Tim says, which is what pushed him to pursue a career in business and finance. But from early on he knew that his natural inclinations made him different: "Since childhood, I always liked to make things with my hands, but that was seen as something done by people who weren't smart. Growing up I always liked the idea of making something. I always liked to cook. Whenever there was an honors section of a course I'd be in it, but when I had the opportunity to take shop in junior high school, I liked it." As a teenager he found that the best and most socially acceptable opportunity to make things was to construct the sets for his high school's theater productions, and he decided to pursue that craft as a career—"not because I loved theater, but just because I wanted to build stuff."

He spent his summers between college terms building sets for shows, but he had so many doubts about his career choice that he switched his major from theater production to theater administration and finally to general business. After graduating from Miami University in Ohio, he took a job as a financial analyst for a large company in keeping with the expectations of his family and their community.

When he was twenty-six, he sat down one evening with a legal pad and tried to write out a plan and a timeline for his life. Since nearly everyone in his family had graduate degrees, he says: "I decided to get an MBA to feel like a complete person. Without a graduate degree, somehow you hadn't fulfilled your destiny." His idea was that he'd work his way up to become the treasurer of a company, and save enough money so he could leave the corporate life at age forty to become a furniture maker. That way, he could afford to live on the much lower pay of his real calling.

After getting his MBA from Indiana University, just as his father had, Tim worked in corporate finance at what he describes as two "blue-blooded banks"—first Manufacturers Hanover Trust and then Barclays, which moved him from Chicago to San Francisco. Still, he was well aware that he was different from his colleagues. "In finance the guys I had worked with would come home after ninety-hour weeks and read the *Wall Street Journal*. I would come home and watch *This Old House.*" When Barclays laid him off at age thirty, he says, "I didn't know what I was going to do. Mostly I wanted to build things." For a while he volunteered at Habitat for Humanity and built homeless shelters, but he explains: "I was really, really lost. I had lost a lot of my confidence. I had a strong pull to make things, but I still had this MBA and there's a huge monetary difference."

During the early to late nineties he scrounged for work at hourly wages from building contractors. He recalls, "I really had just sporadic employment, and I didn't know what I was doing. It was really hard to get over my past." He fell back on his MBA training by working part-time as a financial consultant for a nonprofit organization in Silicon Valley. It was especially difficult for him to commit to woodworking as his full-fledged career when his fellow MBAs in the Bay Area were cashing in during the Internet boom.

In the spring of 2000, Tim decided to make the full-time switch.

He saw a posting on the craigslist website and found a job assembling furniture for the local IKEA store. "After only one or two days I said this is what I have to do—I have to work with tools and my hands," he says. "I'd rather do this than think about corporate finance."

Throughout the difficult decade it took him to transform his life, Tim "received a lot of discouragement" from his family. "My father-in-law was very negative. It was really their own fears, I think, because I was going down-market. Where I grew up, the service people who worked with their hands came in through the back door." He has not been in contact with his parents for years.

Tim uses "divorce" as a metaphor to describe what it has been like for him to finally break with the values and assumptions of the family and the extended community he grew up in. "It's important to divorce yourself from how you were raised and those expectations," he says.

Now, instead of being part of the elite class of business people who own big houses and Porsches and big-screen televisions and take expensive vacations, Tim rents a small one-bedroom apartment and works as a hired manual laborer at the residences of his former peers. "You're sweeping up sawdust in the garage of someone you would have worked with in banking," he says.

Although he's alienated from his erstwhile professional community, estranged from his parents, and even divorced from his wife—their marriage fell apart after he became a full-time woodworker—Tim has thrived. He has become such a master of fine woodworking that he teaches a class in it. He feels content and much more fulfilled by his work now, and he's comfortable with his identity.

A crucial reason why his change has succeeded is the sense of community he's found in the Cole Valley neighborhood where he lives. He's a regular at Tully's café, where a coterie of neighbors linger inside at tables by the storefront picture windows or at the outdoor tables and socialize for an hour or two every morning. He often returns to the café at different times throughout the day when he's in between visits to his clients' sites. The café is a magnet for other people who have also taken risky, unconventional turns in their lives and careers—such as Devon, the mother of two young children who's training to become a police officer, and Katherine, the hospital physician who's developing her craft as a writer. It attracts journalists, artists, photographers, and designers who like to escape from the loneliness of their home offices and enjoy the camaraderie of the informal gathering place where there's almost always someone to talk with no matter what time of day it might be. The neighborhood has plenty of rent-regulated studio apartments as well as larger flats and private houses, and it attracts not only the creative types but also the doctors and medical students from the nearby hospital and the executives and office workers who take the streetcar to skyscrapers downtown. And all of these slices of life wind up meeting at the café and becoming part of a loose and unusually diverse social circle that freely embraces people from widely differing backgrounds, from the mechanic at the garage directly across the street to the neuroscientists up the hill at the UCSF medical school.

"The support network of Cole Valley has been a huge benefit. I'm a very social person and the café has helped me connect with a lot of people," Tim says. "I don't have a support system other than this neighborhood."

How does the framework of "the three keys to change" apply to cases of individuals who overcame self-destructive and life-threatening patterns of thinking, feeling, and acting, such as alcoholism or mental illness? As a reporter I have a persistent nervousness about trying to tell these kinds of true stories about addiction and illness, since it's so difficult to double-check the facts. Information remains shielded by the confidentiality that protects the relationship between doctors and patients. Rehabilitation clinics don't reveal their alumni rosters. There's no way of independently verifying the facts when a doctor talks or writes about a patient whose identity must remain anonymous. Doctors have a tendency to portray themselves as heroic, and patients sometimes romanticize their ordeals.

James Frey was recently discredited for fabricating crucial details in his memoir of alcohol and heroin addiction, *A Million Little Pieces*. Paradoxically, the Frey scandal gave me an idea for approaching the challenge of verifying this type of protected information. Since bestselling memoirs are subject to close scrutiny by critics, reporters, and bloggers, why not look at one that has been in print for several years and retained its reputation for scrupulous honesty? One of the most insightful, compelling, and credible memoirs of our times is writer Caroline Knapp's account of overcoming alcoholism, titled *Drinking: A Love Story*. I've analyzed her story using the "psych concepts" we've covered so far in this book.

PSYCH CONCEPT #1
Frames

As an aspiring writer, Knapp believed that alcohol was a necessary part of a romantic and highly creative life. "I identified with legions of drinking writers," she says, evoking famous literary names such as Dorothy Parker, Dylan Thomas, Eugene O'Neill, William Faulkner, F. Scott Fitzgerald, Ernest Hemingway, and Jack London. "Drinking seemed like part of the turf to me, and there was a hard-edged glamour to writers like that I found deeply attractive. These were . . . people who lived life on a deeper plane than the rest of us, and drinking seemed like a natural outgrowth of their lives and work, both a product of and an antidote to creative angst."

The necessity of drinking was such a deep, unquestioned belief for Knapp that she couldn't conceive of her life without it. She assumed alcohol was vital for her to be sociable, lively, unguarded, and passionate. She thought she was doomed to be "bored and lonely" without it. Even when she began contemplating checking herself into a rehab clinic and becoming sober after two decades of drinking, she writes, "I spent weeks thinking:

"I'll never have fun at a party again.

"I'll never have an intimate conversation again.

"I'll never be able to get married. How can you get married without out Champagne?"

PSYCH CONCEPT #2
Denial and Other Psychological Self-defenses

Even though Knapp had an Ivy League education, the facts didn't set her free. Reading all about addiction and seeing her own blatant symptoms didn't help her because of the overwhelming power of her denial. "When you love somebody, or something," Knapp writes, "it's amazing how willing you are to overlook the flaws." When she was in her thirties, drinking burst the blood vessels near her nose and cheeks, and she would dry heave, and her hands developed tremors that sometimes lasted the entire day. "I did my best to ignore all this," she continues. "I struggled to ignore it, the way a woman hears coldness in a lover's voice and struggles, mightily and knowingly, to misread it. . . . Alcoholics are masters of denial, and I managed to keep whatever worries I harbored about my own drinking nicely compartmentalized, stashed away on the same shelf in my cubicle where I kept my growing collection of books about addiction."

Denial was only one of the many psychological self-defenses that Knapp unconsciously deployed to protect her self-respect. She "projected," too: "Alcoholics are masters at blaming others for the jams they get themselves into," writes Knapp, who describes how she always faulted the personalities of her succession of boyfriends, not the destructive effects of her own uncontrolled drinking, for the problems she had sustaining romantic relationships.

Knapp also relied on avoidance and rationalization to preserve the fragility of her self-esteem. "Alcoholics have notoriously selective memories," she writes. "No matter how sickening the hangover, how humiliating the drunken behavior, how dangerous the blind-drunk drive home, we seem incapable of recalling consistently how bad things got when we drank. . . . When the need or desire to drink becomes too strong, those memories simply evaporate."

Only in her eventual sobriety did Knapp come to realize the full range of rationalization from her drinking years—how she constantly lied to herself as well as to others about the ways alcohol ravaged her life. But Knapp looked back in amazement to realize that even during her many years of denial, "part of me recognized the problem long ago." She adds, "You know and you don't know. Or, more accurately, you know and the part of you that wants no part of this knowledge immediately slips into gear, sliding the fear into a new category." In Alcoholics Anonymous meetings she often heard that "denial is the disease of alcoholism, not just its primary symptom, and it's not hard to see why." There were moments when she did know, with brief clarity, that alcohol was a real problem for her. Sometimes a part of her seemed to remain as an objective observer, looking in the mirror at night and seeing "a depressed, anxious, self-sabotaging thirty-four-year-old woman who could not seem to get out of her own way." And yet, without a sense of hope, Knapp was still powerless to change.

PSYCH CONCEPT #3
Short-term Wins

When she was thirty-four years old, Knapp checked herself into a rehab clinic where there was no possibility of taking a drink. Getting through the first few days proved to her that she *could* get by without alcohol. It was a crucial "short-term win" that broke through her entrenched notions and infused her with a new sense of hope—the belief and expectation that she could live without drinking.

"The hope came from the sheer and simple act of seeing that I could get through twenty-four hours, and then seventy-two and then ninety-six hours, without a drink, something I hadn't done for more than five years," she writes. "I woke up without a hangover my first day, and then the next and the next. I didn't obsess about drinking—where, when, with whom, how much—because the possibility didn't exist, and that felt like liberation to me."

PSYCH CONCEPT #4
The Power of Community and Culture

For Knapp, the first key to change, the "relate" part, was forming a new emotional relationship with the community of fellow alcoholics at a rehabilitation clinic and later at AA meetings back home in Boston. On her first night of rehab, she felt a sense of relief, realizing that her problems "weren't nearly as unique as I thought they were." By her third or fourth night, she wrote to her therapist that she had never felt so much love from people, and she experienced gratitude for the first time in years. Engaged by relationships in this new community, she realized that being sober didn't have to mean being bored and lonely. Her daily AA meetings began to give her the sense of comfort and relief she had found by drinking alcohol. "AA is like a daily shot of hope," she writes. "You see people around you grow and change and flower."

The hope that Knapp felt from her new relationship with a community of recovering alcoholics was what got her through the second key to change, the "repeat" part of learning, practicing, and mastering new habits and skills. As an alcoholic her entire adult life, Knapp really didn't know how to live without alcohol—the countless small skills and daily routines and ways of thinking and acting that enable sober people to thrive in the stress of the world. She writes that AA's twelve steps "seemed to provide a blueprint for living, something I'd always felt I needed and lacked, as though I'd missed some crucial handout years ago in personal conduct class. . . . I was astonished to discover that only one of the twelve steps, the first one, mentions the word *alcohol*. . . . The other eleven all have to do with getting by, learning to be honest and responsible and humble, to ask for help when you need it." In one of the AA lectures she thought, "Oh! So that's how you're supposed to live." Just as Dean Ornish realized that heart patients didn't know how to deal with stress and alienation without smoking, drinking, overeating, or overworking, and just as Mimi Silbert grasped that heroin-addicted third-generation criminals didn't know how to live without drugs, threats, and violence, the AA community realizes that alcoholics simply don't know how to live without alcohol—and proceeds to tell them how and help them practice it until the new habits become second nature.

PSYCH CONCEPT #6
Recasting a Life's Story

When she finally became sober, Knapp needed the third key to change, the "reframing" part—to make sense of her own troubled history in a way that preserved her self-respect. She did this brilliantly by looking at her turbulent twenty-year relationship with alcohol as a sensual "love story," as though she had fallen passionately, even desperately, for an incredibly seductive man who was all wrong for her. "I fell in love and then, because love was ruining everything I cared about, I had to fall out," she writes. Knapp came to see her new sober life as a "divorce" from alcohol, even though part of her was still powerfully lured by it, the way a woman might still feel a strong pull toward a "bad lover" when she finally ends the relationship. The metaphor let Knapp view her previous life as a romantic adventure rather than as a source of only regrets.

•

Looking at Knapp's remarkable story, the crucial questions are still: What finally enabled her to change her own life? What inspired her to take the breakthrough step of checking herself into a rehab clinic? After all, her frames prevented her from conceiving of a life without drinking, and her denial protected her (most of the time, at least) from the truth of her predicament. So what was the initial source of hope? Knapp's breakthrough was wondering whether her view of her life was somehow upside down. She always believed that she drank because she was unhappy. What if it was the other way around and she was unhappy because she drank? "Maybe drinking was, in fact, the problem, not the solution," she realized. That insight led her, two months later, to enter the rehab program and quit drinking.

Psych Concept #9
The "Solution" Might Be the Problem

Unwittingly Knapp had hit upon a simple but extremely useful way of thinking about change that had been pioneered in the 1960s by Drs. Paul Watzlawick, John Weakland, and Richard Fisch at the Brief Therapy Center in Palo Alto, California. When they began their work together, psychotherapy had a reputation for being long and expensive. The process often dragged on for years as doctors tried to understand the causes of patients' problems by looking back to the patients' past histories and exploring traumatic incidents and emotions from their childhoods. But this new team of therapists took a very different approach. "We weren't interested in how a problem got started, just what keeps it going," says Dr. Fisch, a gentle man who's now eighty years old and still working at the Palo Alto center. Their insight was that people kept trying the same things again and again to solve their problems, and that these "attempted solutions" wind up becoming the bigger problem. Rather than acknowledging failure and trying a different approach, people keep doing "more of the same." As Dr. Fisch said, "They just keep doing the same goddamn thing that doesn't work and worsens and perpetuates the problem." Caroline Knapp's story fits into this scenario perfectly: She drank to deal with her unhappiness, but her drinking wound up making her more deeply unhappy and creating new troubles.

Why do people persist in their self-destructive behaviors, ignoring the blatant fact that what they've been doing for many years hasn't solved their problems? They think that they need to do it even more fervently or frequently, as if they were doing the right thing but simply had to try even harder. They continue to do "more of the same."

When alcoholics are miserable, they drink even more. When society puts criminals into our prisons and they come out and commit the same crimes again, we put them back into the same prisons for even longer sentences. When foremen yell at workers on auto assembly lines and it makes the workers rebellious, the foremen yell louder and more frequently.

"Why do they keep doing the same thing?" Fisch asked. "Is it working? No. But what people are doing is 'common sense' to them. People say 'it's the only thing to do.' " In all of these cases their thinking is severely limited by their conceptual frames, their deeply rooted, below-the-surface belief systems. To act any differently would seem to them to be stupid, ridiculous, or even dangerous. If people had told Caroline Knapp that she would actually be less lonely and bored while sober, she wouldn't have believed them, but that's exactly what she wound up discovering once she emerged through rehab and was sustained by AA. If you told criminals that they could learn to thrive in society without drugs, threats, or violence, they wouldn't believe you. If you told GM's executives that trusting their worst workers would result in greater quality and productivity, they would have called you crazy.

Change is a paradoxical process, and trying to change your own life means opening yourself up to new ideas and practices that may seem illogical or even insane to you, at least until you've experienced them for long enough to develop a new understanding. "People will struggle with a problem and not get anywhere and either by desperation or accident they try something different," Dr. Fisch said. "And if they pay attention and stick with it, then that leads to change."

Rather than accidentally arriving at that "something different," why not intentionally make experimentation and learning—the real, hard, frustrating kind prescribed by neuroscientists such as Dr. Michael Merzenich as the key to brain plasticity and fitness—a regular part of your life?

Changing a Loved One

I hesitated when I first called this chapter "Changing a Loved One" because I don't want to imply that we can or should try to make someone change. In the introduction I wrote that one of the biggest misconceptions about change—one of the three Fs, along with "facts" and "fear"—is our reliance on what I call "force," and that includes the powerful emotional pressures that we exert over the people who are close to us. Dr. Dean Ornish likes to say that "people don't resist change, they resist being changed," a one-liner that resounds with wisdom. Every case of profound change we've seen so far in this book has depended on people preserving their self-respect and autonomy even when they're struggling with the most humiliating problems or situations. Their "resistance" is a form of psychological self-defense against the demeaning, condescending, and superior stances of those who assume the knowledge and authority to goad them.

Still, I've stuck with the title "Changing a Loved One" because there's a vital need to know what you can and should do when a parent, a child, a spouse, or a close friend has struggled for a long time with problems and has become demoralized.

This presents a special challenge, since it often means that your relationship with your loved one hasn't helped him or her overcome chronic difficulties—or worse, the relationship, despite your best intentions, may have sustained, complicated, or worsened the root problems. You may be repeating the "attempted solution," doing "more of the same," even though your efforts repeatedly fail to improve the situation.

For example, parents might feel distressed that their grown son has moved back in with them and puts only a lackluster effort into trying to find a job. The parents say they want him to become independent and self-supporting and to have closer relationships with other people. But they spend a load of money finishing the basement and turning it into a comfortable place where he can live rent-free. And they do his laundry, and they play cards with him on Saturday night. It may be very hard for them to recognize or accept that they're part of the problem. Trying to change the way their son thinks, feels, and acts may mean that *they* need to change the way that they think, feel, and act. They may have to "reframe" and realize that kicking their son out of the house and forcing him to support himself is an act of real love rather than a case of reckless endangerment. Only then can they form a *new* (in this case, *renewed)* relationship with him.

Even though we've all heard the word *enabler* countless times in movies and television shows, there's still a natural and powerful urge to "help" friends or family who are troubled—to shield them from the consequences of their actions (or inaction) and to perform tasks that they can and should do by themselves. If we're not *doing* things for them, then we're *telling* them what we think they should do, as if a word from us would shatter their formidable defenses. But the first key to change isn't offering protection or admonition. It's about inspiring hope—the belief and expectation that they can and will change their lives. They need you to *believe* in them, which encourages their own belief. And sometimes they can benefit from being gently led to examples and experiences of other people who've successfully accomplished the change they need to undertake. It usually doesn't help to tell a heart patient to "be healthy," but it's useful to introduce that heart patient to people who've suffered from the same illness and overcome it.

An example of the impact of inspiring hope in others so they can change can be found in Kay Redfield Jamison's memoir *An Unquiet Mind.* Jamison had been "intensely emotional" as a child growing up in a military family. She was "severely depressed" as an adolescent, and her first attack of manic-depressive illness came when she was a senior in high school. Even when she was studying for her PhD in psychiatry at the University of California at Los Angeles, she writes, "I still did not make any connection in my own mind between the problems I had experienced and what was described as manic-depressive illness in the textbooks. In a strange reversal of medical-student syndrome, where students become convinced that they have whatever disease it is they are studying, I blithely went on with my clinical training and never put my mood swings into any medical context whatsoever. When I look back on it, my denial and ignorance seem virtually incomprehensible."

In 1974, three months after becoming an associate professor at UCLA, Jamison went "ravingly psychotic." In the fall she was prescribed lithium, which was the most effective medicine for her condition at that time. Her family and friends expected her to be obedient, but by the following spring she had defied her doctor and the people who loved her and stopped taking the pills. She was powerfully addicted to the high moods of her manic phases—"their intensity, euphoria, assuredness, and their infectious ability to induce high moods and enthusiasms in other people"—even though the down phases imperiled her.

One of Jamison's first steps toward change was inspired when she fell in love with David, a handsome officer in the British Army Medical Corps. While she was recovering from a "long suicidal depression," David asked her to stay with him in London. She writes, "His belief in me, in who I was, and in my basic health . . . pushed back the nightmare fears of unpredictable moods and violence. It must have been clear to David that I despaired of ever returning to my normal self, because he set about, in his rather systematic way, to reassure me." He quickly arranged dinners for them with two senior British army officers who led steady lives even though they were manic-depressive. The officers were smart, charming, elegant, self-assured, and entertaining. "At no time during either of the dinner parties was manic-depressive illness discussed," Jamison writes. "It was, in fact, the very normality of the evenings that was so reassuring and so important to me. Being introduced to such 'normal' men, both from a world much like the one I had known as a child, was one of David's many intuitive acts of kindness."

Jamison's psychiatrist also proved to be a model of how to help another person who's struggling with change: "I remember sitting in his office a hundred times during those grim months and each time thinking, What on earth can he say that will make me feel better or keep me alive? Well, there never was anything he could say; that's the funny thing. It was all the stupid, desperately optimistic, condescending things he didn't say that kept me alive; all the compassion and warmth I felt from him that could not have been said . . . and his granite belief that my life was worth living." The way her psychiatrist acted would have been exemplary for a family member or a friend as well.

•

The first key to change is forming a new emotional relationship, which often means meeting a new person who serves as a source of hope for you. What if your loved one forms a new relationship with *someone else*? That may seem an uncomfortable idea, but it doesn't mean your spouse will divorce you or your child won't call you anymore. It might mean that you have to accept another person who exerts a powerful influence in the loved one's life—whether that person is a mentor, teacher, trainer, guru, colleague, or friend. Instead of feeling threatened by this new relationship, you can try to become allied with it.

This idea brings to mind the story of an American family in which the mother had a very close bond with her son. She had spent her life as a philanthropic leader, yet their relationship never inspired him to be much of a philanthropist himself, even though he had become quite wealthy early in his adulthood. When he fell in love with a woman and eventually married her, his mother could have felt threatened by this new rival for his attention and affection. Instead she realized that the wife could be a very effective ally for encouraging her son to change.

Meet the family of the world's richest man. . . .

THE CHANGE SCENARIO:
The Gates Family

When you're the richest person in the world, worth tens of billions of dollars, there aren't many peers who can serve as your role models. Bill Gates, who usually ranks as the world's wealthiest individual, has enjoyed a long friendship with Warren Buffett, who often ranks as the second wealthiest. Buffett is considerably older and serves as something of a father figure for the software mogul.

So, in the early nineties, when reporters pressed Gates about his plans for philanthropy, his response was not surprising. Buffett had already declared he was going to give away nearly all of his money and the cause that interested him the most was "population control," which means encouraging families to have fewer children. When Gates said exactly the same things, it looked as though he was simply emulating the example of his close friend, bridge partner, and fellow decabillionaire.

I covered Gates when I was a reporter for *Fortune* in those years. I interviewed him a number of times and went to many of his public appearances and got to know his oldest friends and closest colleagues. But I never heard Gates or any of the people close to him say anything that would suggest he was actually interested in philanthropy. Gates's official pronouncement was that he wasn't going to give away his money until he had retired from full-time work at Microsoft, and no one thought there was any chance of that happening for decades. Gates was still in his thirties, and he was a workaholic, and the company he ran was an extension of his own ego.

Gates's statements suggested that Microsoft consumed too

much of his time and energy for him to give proper attention to philanthropy. Granted, he was deeply engaged by his work, but that didn't prevent him from dedicating time to challenging intellectual pursuits. He was fascinated by science, for example, and for fun he liked watching videotapes of lectures about advanced physics by the Nobel laureate Richard Feynman.

The truth wasn't that Gates didn't have time for philanthropy; it was that he lacked interest and enthusiasm. The fear of backlash from public opinion and the press, which cast him as extraordinarily greedy, didn't sway him. Nor did the fear of reprisal from government regulators who believed that Gates was too powerful and were trying to break up his company. It was obvious that hoarding his wealth was a serious public relations problem. But by saying that he would give away money *someday,* when he retired, he was defending his self-respect through "avoidance," one of the most common forms of unconscious psychological self-defense.

KEY #1

Relate

Gates's mother seizes on his new emotional relationship with his fiancée Melinda to inspire hope for change.

●

The people with the most powerful emotional influence on Gates were his longtime girlfriend, Melinda French, who had been a manager at Microsoft, and his mother, Mary, with whom he had always been very close. Gates became engaged to French when his mother was dying from breast cancer. The night before their wedding, Mary wrote a letter to Melinda. As Michael Specter reported in the *New Yorker:* "She stressed the great opportunities the two would have as a couple to improve the world—and the unique responsibilities that came with immense wealth. 'It was really quite beautiful,' Melinda said. 'And that was what got us going.' "

Mary Gates didn't try to "force" Bill to become a philanthropist through the pressures of scolding or shaming. Her message conveyed her belief and expectation that Bill and his new wife would achieve great things together. And the message came at a very emotional time (their wedding and her fatal illness), which surely amplified its power and resonance.

Bill's interest in population control ultimately led him and Melinda to look into issues of public health. They learned that treatable diseases, such as diarrhea, were killing millions of people every year. "The whole thing was stunning to us," Gates said. "We couldn't even believe it. You think in philanthropy that your dollars will just be marginal, because the really juicy obvious things will all have been taken. So you look at this stuff and we are like, wow! When somebody is saying that we can save many lives for hundreds of dollars each, the answer has to be no, no, no. That would already have been done. . . . We really did think it was too shocking to be true." The facts didn't fit his frame, and his instinct was to reject the facts as crazy or unbelievable.

It turned out that a big reason why Gates had shrunk away from philanthropy was *demoralization*—the sense that the situation was hopeless and he was powerless because even his billions of dollars wouldn't have much of an impact. But the positive emotional persuasion of his mother and his wife had led him to explore the situation more closely, and this new information inspired his belief and expectation of success.

KEY #1 AND KEY #3
Relate and Reframe

The final step in Gates's transformation came when he embraced a new way of thinking. The turning point took place during a dinner party that the couple threw at their lakeside home for prominent scientists who specialized in public health. "We were both extraordinarily impressed by their knowledge, their expertise, their desire to solve problems," Melinda said. "And toward the end of the dinner Bill posed the question: 'If you had more money, what would you do?' and the room came alive. Just to hear what their ideas were was so exciting for us. It was a revelation. And we both walked away from that dinner thrilled, because we had been surrounded by people that were so brilliant at Microsoft. And we saw immediately that these were the same type of people."

Bill Gates loved being around people he considered brilliant. Microsoft had thousands of employees and several dozen buildings on a sprawling campus in the Seattle suburbs, and Gates could have put his own office anywhere he wanted, but he didn't put it in a building with the company's top businesspeople. He decided to work among Microsoft's top researchers, who were typically former professors and had terrific intellectual firepower and worked on the biggest technological challenges. Those were the people he was excited to talk with. They were one of the greatest reasons why he kept working full-time at Microsoft even after the company achieved domination of the market. Once the idea of philanthropy was "reframed" in Gates's mind and went from being a burdensome moral obligation to being a way of engaging in intellectual challenges with geniuses, he was really sold on it.

The couple donated $20 billion to their foundation, making it the world's richest, and they began funding astonishing improvements in global health.

Changing Your Company, Organization, or Societal Institution

We've seen how the three keys to change can transform the lives of individuals. In this chapter my goal is to show how the same tools can create profound change in the cultures of organizations and institutions. After all, a company is no more than a bunch of people united by common practices, beliefs, and "frames."

I've covered business for the past two decades as a reporter for magazines such as *Fortune* and *Fast Company,* and the two most impressive corporate transformations that I've seen have taken place at Apple and at IBM. Apple is an unusual case because the first key to change, the "relate" part, involved the company's employees and customers renewing a relationship rather than forming a new one. The turnaround came about when Steve Jobs, Apple's cofounder, returned as its leader after an absence of a decade and restored the innovative culture that he had helped to create in the company's formative years. The remarkable story is the subject of my book, *The Second Coming of Steve Jobs.*

But the IBM story is even more intriguing and instructive in many ways. Recently when Sir Howard Stringer became the new chief executive officer of Sony, a once great corporation that was struggling to reinvent itself, he sought guidance from Louis Gerstner, the chief executive officer who saved IBM from possible collapse in the nineties.

The IBM story has gotten even better in the four years since Gerstner handed over the leadership there. IBM's cultural transformation remains very much an ongoing process, one that I had an extraordinary opportunity to study close-up when I was granted access to some of the top executives who are leading it. If IBM, a company with decades of entrenched culture and hundreds of thousands of employees around the world, can pull off a major change, then there's hope for any company, organization, or institution of lesser size and scope.

THE "CHANGE OR DIE" SCENARIO
International Business Machines Corp.

In the 1960s a man named Thomas Watson Jr., who was the chief executive officer of IBM, moved the company's headquarters from the epicenter of Manhattan to an old apple orchard about thirty miles to the north. His reason was that he wanted his company to survive a nuclear attack on New York City. Nothing else seemed threatening to the colossal corporation. IBM was so powerful and invulnerable that only an intercontinental ballistic missile could bring about its demise, or so everyone thought. Seven of every ten dollars spent on computers went to IBM, and the rest were fought over by a bunch of rivals known as the "seven dwarfs." IBM made more money than any other company in the world. The math was simple: IBM sold big computers, so-called *mainframes,* the size of refrigerators, for $4 million apiece and kept $3 million of that price as profit. IBM had plenty of other businesses, but it made an easy $4 billion a year in profits just from those big boxes.

The company could afford to be very generous to its 400,000 worldwide employees. The policy was that everyone would have jobs there for life. IBM had never laid off anyone. It was an extremely proud company. When executives throughout American business were surveyed, they named IBM as the company they most admired. *Fortune* magazine called Watson "the greatest capitalist in history."

The technocrats at IBM were in a better position than just about anyone to see the future of their industry. And see it they did. In the early 1980s IBM's engineers began circulating reports predicting that the costly, big computers would be replaced by networks of cheaper, small computers, and that the company had to change in response to a changing world. But no one really *believed* that IBM could change so profoundly. Just as we commonly believe that people don't change, we also believe that big organizations don't change. So the most talented and thoughtful individuals at IBM saw all the trouble that was coming, and they began to leave the company that no one ever left. Just how many of them fled? That's easy to figure: IBM ranked all its employees from one to five, with one as the highest grade. Only one tenth of IBM's workforce in the

United States—22,000 out of 220,000 people—received a one. In 1986, IBM offered early retirement, with lucrative severance packages, to ten thousand volunteers, and it lost eight thousand of the "ones." The smartest people took the first good chance to get out of there.

IBM's momentum carried it forward for a while longer. In 1990 the company began the new decade by turning a profit of $6 billion for the year. But then, suddenly, IBM began to collapse. Rivals were selling "workstations" that cost less than $100,000 and fit on top of a desk. These smaller computers had gotten so fast and so useful that it didn't make sense anymore for customers to pay a king's ransom for IBM's hulking refrigerators. In desperation IBM reduced the prices on its big machines by 50 percent, then by 70 percent, but it still didn't matter. In 1992 IBM lost $5 billion. It was the largest sum of money that any corporation had ever lost in a single year. As IBM's stock price fell from $43 to $12, its shareholders lost a total of $75 billion.

IBM's top executives worried that there wouldn't be enough cash to "make payroll." They ended the policy of lifetime employment and began to lay off 140,000 workers. The remaining employees were dazed and demoralized. Outside experts said that IBM's "brand" was worse than worthless: The IBM name, once glorious, was so sullied that it was actually hurting the company. The investment bankers and stock traders who run Wall Street figured that IBM was dying. *Break it up and sell off the pieces,* they advised. The company's board of directors rushed to hire a new chief executive officer to be a "change master" and try to save the place. But it looked as though no prominent business leader would take the position because they all believed that IBM was doomed. "Who'd

Want This Job?" asked a headline on the front page of the *Wall Street Journal*.

KEY #1
Relate

Employees form an emotional relationship with a new leader who inspires their belief that they can change and their expectation that they will change.

•

But one man came forward and volunteered. His name was Louis V. Gerstner Jr., and he had already run American Express and Nabisco. Gerstner's first day in his new role as the head of IBM was April 2, 1993. At the time IBM had its own internal television network that broadcast to thousands of television sets located throughout its factories, offices, and laboratories around the world. Gerstner decided to record a video for all the employees to watch. He went in front of the camera and read a script prepared by the company's public relations people. But it didn't feel right. He turned to his advisers and asked, "Can I try one on my own?"

This time, Gerstner spoke his own words: "IBM was and will again be the world's most successful company."

Gerstner wasn't photogenic. He wasn't a smoothly polished speaker. He didn't have the charm or charisma of other business leaders. For a guy with two Ivy League degrees, he was still kind of gruff. He wasn't slick at all, but he came across as sincere. He actually *believed* what he was saying. And that was the beginning of IBM's revival.

Never before had Lou Gerstner needed to deal with the "common people." Ever since college he had always been in the company of the elite, and they respected and admired him for his exceptional intellect. After earning an engineering degree from Dartmouth and an MBA from Harvard Business School, he went to work at the age of twenty-three for McKinsey & Co., the consulting firm that tells the world's business leaders what to do. McKinsey hires the top students not just from America's MBA programs but also from PhD programs in many countries. Still Gerstner stood out for his ability to cut his way through massive amounts of information. He became a partner at the firm in just five years, which was faster than anyone had ever earned that coveted promotion. He was named the firm's youngest senior partner. Then he went from advising the top people in business to being one of the top people himself.

As the head of American Express, Gerstner was a boss in the Theory X mode. "What people at American Express remember most about Gerstner was how much he managed through intimidation," wrote *Wall Street Journal* reporter Paul Carroll. "Through the closed door of his office, he might be heard yelling, 'That's the stupidest thing I've ever heard! You're an idiot! Get out of my office.' . . . One subordinate says that knees buckled and hands trembled when Gerstner walked into a room." While Gerstner's temper was legendary, so was his toughness and tenacity. Even after he lost two fingers in a lawn mower accident, he showed up for work the next day.

When Gerstner took over IBM, everyone thought he would be fixated on what had worked for him throughout his career as a

McKinsey consultant: purely intellectual analysis and strategy. They thought he would try to revive the company through financial maneuvers such as selling assets and cutting costs. But somehow Gerstner intuitively grasped that those tools wouldn't be nearly enough. He needed to transform the entrenched corporate culture. That meant changing the attitudes and behaviors of hundreds of thousands of employees who were demoralized by the company's failure. In his memoir, *Who Says Elephants Can't Dance?*, Gerstner writes that he realized he needed to make a powerful emotional appeal to get the colleagues "to believe in themselves again—to believe that they had the ability to determine their own fate." He needed to "shake them out of their depressed stupor, remind them of who they were—you're IBM, damn it!" Rather than sitting in a corner office negotiating deals and analyzing spreadsheets, he needed to convey his belief and his passion through hundreds of hours of personal appearances.

Gerstner was still brittle and imperious in private. A decade later IBM employees still tell this anecdote: One day Gerstner was walking on the treadmill at the gym at the company's headquarters when he took a call on his cell phone. The noise of the other treadmills and the stair-climbers made it difficult for Gerstner to focus on his conversation, so he shouted "Silence!" and the rest of the executives halted their workouts.

Gerstner wasn't naturally charming, but when he made his appeal to IBM's huge workforce, he proved to be an engaging and emotional public speaker. A *New York Times* reporter followed one of Gerstner's barnstorming campaigns in 1994 and saw that Gerstner could be "an impassioned orator." Gerstner said that the culture was "not something you do by writing memos. You've got to appeal to people's emotions. They've got to buy in with their hearts and their bellies, not just their minds."

That kind of emotional persuasion isn't what they teach at business schools. Gerstner says he never once heard the word *passion* mentioned in a Harvard classroom. And it doesn't come naturally to the technocrats who run things—the engineers, scientists, lawyers, doctors, accountants, and managers who pride themselves on rational, disciplined thinking. But it's essential.

"Behavior change happens mostly by speaking to people's feelings," says John Kotter, who has spent decades studying leadership and change in the corporate realm. "This is true even in organizations that are focused on analysis and measurement, even among people who think of themselves as smart in an MBA sense. In highly successful change efforts, people find ways to help others see the problems or solutions in ways that influence emotions, not just thought."

KEY #2 AND KEY #3
Repeat and Reframe

IBM's senior executives form a new emotional relationship with a new mentor who helps them learn new habits and skills as well as new ways of thinking.

●

It was one thing for Lou Gerstner to inspire his people to believe that IBM could change. It was quite another for him to get them to assimilate new ways.

In 1999, six years after taking over as the company's chief executive, Gerstner was working at home on a Sunday. Reading a monthly report from one of IBM's many "business units," Gerstner found a line, buried deep, saying that the executives had decided to save money in the current quarter—the three-month period when the profits or losses are reported—by abruptly curtailing the company's efforts in a promising new area.

Gerstner was incensed. How often did this happen? He was so outraged that he immediately wrote a memo. When his colleagues read it, they knew that Gerstner had written it himself in a fury because of the abundance of typographical errors.

He asked his senior vice president of strategy, J. Bruce Harreld, to look into the issue. Harreld had been brought to IBM by Gerstner himself, and for a good reason. He had a much more entrepreneurial mentality than the veteran IBM executives, who were used to being part of a mammoth corporation that had been around for decades. Harreld had helped launch Boston Market, a chain of rotisserie chicken restaurants, and turn it into a national success while he was there.

Harreld looked into the matter for Gerstner and found a similar pattern across the board, which he documented with twenty-two case studies. IBM had plenty of new ideas—its famous research labs won thousands of patents a year—but it had a remarkably hard time turning those ideas into new businesses. IBM had come up with many crucial inventions but then watched while others, such as Oracle and Cisco, built huge companies around them and earned billions of dollars.

What were the root causes of this frustrating situation? The main problem, Harreld realized, was that IBM focused on protecting what it already had. The company rewarded executives for the short-term results from their tried-and-true businesses. The leaders were reluctant to devote attention, resources, time, or talent to rolling the dice. "Everything was based on the current period, not on the future," says David Dobson, who was Harreld's deputy strategist.

Neither Gerstner nor Harreld spent much time on new businesses, and they didn't tap their "A-team" of executives to run them. "We were relegating this to the most inexperienced people," Harreld says. "We were not putting the best and brightest talent on this." Their most seasoned and capable executives took care of the big, old, established businesses that account for today's sales and profits, not the risky new efforts that represent the company's growth and its future. And that had to change.

So Harreld helped create a program called Emerging Business Opportunities (EBOs). The idea was that he would reassign some of those star executives. Their new jobs would be starting new businesses from scratch, and Harreld would serve as their tutor throughout the difficult process.

Harreld was the perfect guy to instruct his fellow IBM executives about entrepreneurship, which involves a new set of habits and skills for them as well as a different mindset. He was a former entrepreneur and also an engaging, experienced teacher—he used to be a professor at the Harvard Business School and at Northwestern University's Kellogg School of Management.

For starters Harreld needed a "short-term win" to prove the potential of his plan. So he decided to begin with one executive as a guinea pig for the great experiment. And the man he tapped was named Rod Adkins.

Rod Adkins couldn't understand why his career seemed to be taking such a sudden and devastating blow. Up until then, he was the epitome of a hotshot executive at IBM. In a culture where your status is determined largely by how many people you have working under you and how much revenue they produce, Adkins was a star. He ran a division with 35,000 employees and $4 billion in annual sales. If his division were broken off as a stand-alone company, it would have been one of the largest companies in America.

Then, one day, the brass summarily stripped him of all that status and power. They reassigned him to a business that didn't produce any revenue. It didn't even really exist yet. It was just a weird idea. And now he had no one reporting to him. It looked as though this move might be the company's way of letting a senior executive know that he was no longer wanted there.

"Geez," Adkins said. "What do I tell my mom?"

"He thought he was fired," recalls Bruce Harreld, who had to bring IBM's president, Sam Palmisano, to talk to Adkins personally and reassure him of his importance to the company. If anything, Adkins had actually been promoted, but that was difficult for him to grasp because the new culture that Gerstner and Harreld were trying to instill was such a shocking departure from the company's long-entrenched ways. The facts didn't fit his frame.

What they wanted Adkins to do was actually much harder than running a multibillion-dollar operation. It was creating one totally from scratch. And that's exactly what Adkins accomplished. Three years later, in 2003, his new venture had already revved up to annual sales of $2.4 billion.

Bruce Harreld promised IBM's board of directors that EBOs would create $2 billion of new revenue every year. The actual results wildly surpassed all expectations. In the program's first four years, IBM launched twenty-five EBOs. Three failed and were closed down, but the remaining twenty-two thrived and brought in annual revenues of $15 billion.

"Through EBOs, IBM has become more of a learning organization," says Caroline Kovac, who built a new $1 billion, thousand-employee business from scratch. "We've become more willing to experiment, more willing to accept failure, learn from it, and move on. It's more a part of our culture. It's really a profound change. Now being an EBO leader is a really desirable job at IBM." Harreld says he doesn't even have to recruit EBO leaders anymore: "Today I have my peers coming to me and offering to run these."

Harreld holds what amount to private tutorials on starting and running business ventures. He meets one-on-one with each EBO leader for three or four hours a month. At first the process is confusing and difficult for the transplanted executive, who's still stuck in the mindset of running an established division. "It takes me and them four months at least to stop the crap," Harreld explains. "In an established business it's all about keeping things under control. These guys are so buttoned up. You bring them into a new business area, and it's almost hilarious." When Adkins embarked on his new venture, he showed up at his first few monthly meetings and Harreld would ask, "What problems are you having?" and Adkins would insist that there were no problems. *No problems!* New businesses are *all about* problems.

"Rod came from a culture where the senior managers feel they're expected to know all the answers to all the questions and deal with the issues themselves," explains Gary Cohen, who helped Harreld run the EBO program. "You understand a mature business because it has a level of predictability. But with an EBO, there's a lot you don't know, and you have to discover, learn, and adjust." That's what change is all about.

When Harreld lectures his colleagues about change, he starts off by showing a slide with the following list of famous brands:

> *Levi Strauss*
> *Kodak*
> *Zenith*
> *Firestone*
> *Timex*
> *Nestlé*
> *U.S. Steel*
> *Polaroid*
> *Sears*
> *IBM*

"What do these companies have in common?" he asks. "They all used to lead their industries. These are companies that were in trouble for a long time. Did they know they were in trouble? Absolutely. But there's enormous inertia. The culture gets hardened to make things stay the way they are."

Harreld flashes a slide with a picture of a brick wall and all the things that bounce off it when leaders try to change the cultures of their companies: speeches, three-ring binders, wall charts, conference handouts, Lucite cubes.

"There are probably a hundred books on culture and they all miss the concept and make it too complex," he says. "I have four kids. How do they learn to behave? They watch their parents, and later they watch others whom they respect. Inside a company, people are the same way." Rod Adkins was well respected by the other senior executives, and Harreld made a conspicuous example out of him knowing that his peers would emulate him.

•

A dozen years after IBM nearly collapsed, the company is much more innovative and willing to take risks. Its annual profits rebounded to more than $8 billion in 2004, and its stock price revived from $12 to $80 and higher. It has hired many new people: Most of its 325,000 employees have been there for no more than five years, so the new regime is the only one they've known. But cultures are incredibly persistent, and Bruce Harreld and Sam Palmisano (who succeeded Lou Gerstner as chief executive in 2002) are still striving to change IBM's culture and realize the vision of being the world's most successful company again.

The company held several worldwide virtual meetings over the Internet, called "culture jams," that revealed many people near the bottom of the hierarchy were frustrated because they didn't have the authority to make decisions on their own. They needed to get prior approval for seemingly everything. They couldn't book their own airfares if they needed to travel on short notice to solve business problems. One of Palmisano's advisers, John Iwata, suggested setting aside five thousand dollars for each of IBM's lowest-level managers to spend at their own discretion, no questions asked.

"Great, let's do it," Palmisano said. "Talk to the controller and the CFO [chief financial officer] so I can announce it tomorrow."

When Iwata spoke with the money guys, "their jaws dropped," he recalls. IBM had thirty thousand managers. That meant letting people spend $150 million without the company having any idea where the money was going.

"We need to put in the proper controls," they said.

"No," said Palmisano. "This is trust. This is a hundred and fifty million dollar bet on trust."

So they made the announcement and the managers started calling headquarters and asking, "What approvals do we need?" They couldn't accept the fact that they were being trusted to spend money. The fact didn't fit their frame, so they hardly touched the funds that were set aside. After one year, only $100,000 of the $150 million had been spent.

IBM's top executives were walking the walk—they didn't just talk about pushing down authority, they put up the money and officially changed the company's policies to enable it to happen. But you need to walk the walk for a long time before your actions really change the way that people think, feel, and act. After years or decades of experiencing the old ways, people aren't going to believe you when you tell them that things are different now, even if they really are different. People need to experience it first. It's not enough for the chief executive officer to say that he wants senior executives to take big risks and start new businesses. The senior executives need to see that their colleague Rod Adkins actually started one—and that he was recognized and rewarded by the company's top brass for his efforts. It's not enough to say that you want the frontline managers to spend money without asking for your approval. The frontline managers need to see that someone down the hall made an independent decision to charter a private plane to fly out to help a customer in an emergency—and got promoted, not fired, for the move. Our beliefs—the frames embedded in our unconscious minds—are formed through repeated experience over time, and usually they can be reshaped only by experience.

BONUS MINI CASE STUDY
Changing the Schools
Knowledge Is Power Program (KIPP)

America's public schools have been in decline and crisis for so long that many people have given up hope and dismissed the situation as impossible to fix. But there's a nationwide chain of charter schools—free schools funded by taxes but run by entrepreneurial organizations—that is achieving extraordinary results by applying the three keys to change.

The Knowledge is Power Program (KIPP) was started in 1994 by two public school teachers in Houston, Mike Feinberg and Dave Levin. By 2006 KIPP (which rhymes with flip) was running forty-six schools with around nine thousand students overall. The kids come from poor neighborhoods: 75 percent of the students are eligible for the federally subsidized school lunch program. And they're overwhelmingly from minority groups: 90 percent are African American or Latino.

KIPP doesn't pick the better students from among the regular public schools run by the city school systems—it accepts students regardless of their previous history of grades and conduct. And the Kippsters, as they're known, start out with all the disadvantages of their counterparts in the public schools. Most of KIPP's schools run from the fifth to eighth grades, and when the kids enter the program as fifth graders, their average reading and math scores are at the 28th percentile, meaning that they perform worse than 72 percent of American kids and as good or better than only 28 percent. But by the time they're ready to graduate from eighth grade, the Kippsters' scores have shot up to the 74th percentile, which ranks them ahead of many of America's more affluent school districts. That's simply a fantastic achievement.

Overwhelmingly KIPP's eighth grade graduates go on to attend outstanding "magnet" public high schools, which serve the best students from around the city, or they receive scholarships to attend the most prestigious private high schools, including such elite institutions as Exeter and Andover. Their KIPP education makes them twice as likely to go to college. In Houston and New York, the two cities where KIPP first opened schools, only 48 percent of the public high school seniors go on to college; in comparison, 80 percent of the Kippsters have been accepted to college. It's no wonder the *Washington Post* wrote that "KIPP appears to be the most interesting and successful attempt so far to raise the achievements of low-income, minority children."

How does KIPP do it? The principals and the teachers often take creative approaches. They're given a lot of freedom by the national KIPP foundation. That has made it difficult for outside observers to figure out the real secret behind its success. Much of the media coverage has focused on the few things that all the KIPP schools have in common, especially the long hours: Students have to be at school from 7:30 in the morning until 5:00 in the afternoon on weekdays, and they attend classes for four hours on Saturdays as well as for a month during what used to be their summer vacation. Plus they're given at least two hours of homework every night. The numbers add up: In the course of a year, Kippsters spend 1,878 hours in school, which is 62 percent longer than the 1,170 hours their peers spend in city-run public schools in the same neighborhoods. For the teachers, working at KIPP demands great commitment: They even give out their cell phone numbers so students can call in the evenings with questions about homework.

The long hours are obviously important, but the facts still don't explain the underlying psychology: What motivates both students and teachers to put in the extra time, energy, and effort? Why not choose to stay in more traditional schools that are far less demanding?

What's really happening is that KIPP has hit on the three keys of change, especially the first key: relate. KIPP creates a new relationship between students and teachers that inspires a new sense of hope. From the start the program strives to inspire in students the desire to go to college and the belief and expectation that they will go. For minority kids from families with low incomes, this is a new outlook: Before enrolling at KIPP some of these kids don't know anyone who had gone to college, and their parents and teachers don't expect that they will go either and don't hold that up as an aspiration.

Sometimes their first contact with KIPP revolves around the astonishing notion that they can go to college. When KIPP was getting ready to open its first school in San Francisco, its teachers went to the parking lots of shopping malls to recruit students with that very pitch.

When students enter fifth grade, they're typically ten years old, which is still eight years away from when they can enter college and twelve years from when they'd likely graduate. But their fifth grade class is identified by the year that those students will graduate from universities. If you entered KIPP as a fifth grader in the fall of 2007, then you would constantly hear the teachers and principal talk about you and your classmates as belonging to "the Class of 2019" instead of calling you "the fifth grade." Your classroom would be named after the university attended by your teacher—"Harvard," for example, or "Stanford," which are the kinds of places you're expected to get into.

The written statement of KIPP's philosophy is called "The Five Pillars," and the first of the pillars is high expectations, and boy, do they mean it. I think the biggest reason for KIPP's phenomenal success is that the teachers communicate their sincere belief in the students, which inspires the students' hopes for going to college. That sense of hope motivates the commitment of time and energy that the children need to put into their studies. All good schools rely on the second and third keys to change—school is all about learning new skills and new ways of thinking—but KIPP has really mastered the vital first key.

The teachers don't just say it's important for their pupils to excel and go on to college; they sacrifice much of their personal lives to make it happen. The teachers really show that they have a deep commitment to the success of their students, and that helps to transform the relationship and infuse it with emotional power.

Changing Your Industry

In our current technological age, sometimes an entire industry finds itself facing a change or die crisis. Even though the many executives at the rival companies are well aware of the facts of the situation, and they are driven by the fear of losing market share, profits, and ultimately their own lucrative positions, they still stubbornly resist change—until they form a relationship with someone who can inspire and teach them about new ways for the business.

That's what happened to the advertising industry when it was threatened by the Internet revolution in the late 1990s and early 2000s. It's a classic example of how a culture can become entrenched not just within a single company or organization but also throughout an entire major industry—and how that culture can change dramatically in a short time.

THE CHANGE OR DIE SCENARIO
The Advertising Industry

In his first job right out of Yale's graduate school in 1965, Peter Sealey was responsible for buying television ads for Duncan Hines cake mixes. It was a pretty simple job, actually. If he bought three thirty-second commercial spots during the soap operas on daytime television, he could be sure that four out of five American women between the ages of eighteen and forty-nine would see the ads and know about the new Double Dutch Fudge flavor that his company, Procter & Gamble, had just launched. What's more, he could place the ads on soap operas owned by P&G itself, which made the deals rather cozy.

Through the sixties, seventies, eighties, and into the nineties, large companies hired many young executives like Sealey whose enviable jobs were to buy ads on network television shows and then go out for expense-account lunches at fancy restaurants. It was a great gig, and they wanted it to go on and on. There was only one problem: Fewer and fewer people were watching those ads and hearing the jingles. Housewives joined the workforce and weren't around to tune in to daytime shows. The videocassette recorder made it commonplace for viewers to tape their favorite sitcoms and skip the commercials. Cable TV became popular. The Internet suddenly turned into a national obsession. Digital video recorders made it even easier to record shows and zap out the ads. The television audience diminished, and what was left got sliced dozens of ways. There wasn't much of a mass audience anymore for the mass marketers.

By the mid-nineties, the big advertisers were faced with a change or die crisis. The viewers who remained loyal to the broadcast television networks were the consumers in whom they were the least interested. Advertisers wanted to reach the younger, more affluent, and better educated parts of America, but the people who clung to free television were the oldest, poorest, and least educated, the ones who couldn't afford cable or still didn't want to figure out how to program their VCRs.

The situation was weirdly paradoxical: Prime-time ratings were falling by two percent every year, but the networks were charging more and more for the advertisers to reach this smaller and less desirable audience. Over the eighties and nineties the cost of a prime-time ad on ABC *quadrupled,* from five dollars per thousand viewers to twenty dollars. That was twice the rate of inflation. The networks got away with it because the ad executives still needed some way to put their messages across to a big audience, and television was the only way they knew how to do it. One prominent media expert, Nicholas Donatiello, said: "These advertisers are like drug addicts: As ads are less effective, they have to buy more and more to get the same fix." While Peter Sealey had been able to reach 80 percent of American women with three commercials, now companies could buy dozens of television ads and still, most people wouldn't know about the new flavors they were introducing.

After many years of denial, the ad execs briefly faced up to the crisis. Tens of millions of consumers—especially the young, affluent, technocratic ones—were spending their time on the Web using search engines such as Yahoo! and Google. So the execs began buying ads on the Internet. But the people who ran the major advertising agencies in New York didn't like the new medium. These mature Madison Avenue types loathed dealing with Silicon Valley youngsters who had an arrogant edge even though they were only twenty-two years old and had no experience whatsoever in the ad business. The younger Internet crowd was heady with the idea of creating a new order, and was condescending to the grown-ups of the old establishment; they counted on using facts and fear to motivate sales, rather than trying to develop rapport and trust with the veterans.

Then, in 2001, when the stock prices of Internet start-ups collapsed and it looked like the Internet might have been a hyped-up fad, many of the Madison Avenue types openly gloated. They were relieved that the media business might not have to change much after all. They went back into denial, believing that they could still win awards for their thirty-second television commercials rather than having to learn how to promote brands through an unfamiliar new medium. Internet ad sales fell 25 percent from 2000 to 2002 and looked like they might be heading straight back toward irrelevance.

But Peter Sealey saw what was happening. He had become a business professor at Stanford and Berkeley, and he began giving a speech titled "The Death of Ad-Supported TV." Television commercials had become so costly and ineffective that the companies that bought them needed to take out the blame on someone. So the life of a chief marketing officer had become "nasty, brutish, and short," he said. On average these executives lasted only twenty-three months in their jobs at any company. In the food industry, where Sealey started his career, the marketing chiefs typically lasted only twelve months. "CMOs have the life expectancy of a tourist in Baghdad," he said.

KEY #1
Relate

Advertising executives form a new relationship with Wenda Harris Millard, who inspires new hope.

●

The ad execs needed someone to make them believe and expect that they could make the jump from television to the Internet and to help them learn the new skills and new ways of thinking that would enable them to pull it off.

That person, it turned out, was Wenda Harris Millard.

The Madison Avenue executives liked Millard because she wasn't a kid from Silicon Valley. She didn't act like a teenager—she was fifty years old, the mother of two teenagers, and lived in the suburbs in Connecticut. She took the Metro North commuter train to work (what could be more old school?) at an office tower near Grand Central Station. She was a regular at the "power lunch" restaurants where New York's advertising and media executives loved to schmooze: Michael's, the Four Seasons, and Lever House, where the maître d' would greet her warmly by her first name and escort her to a prime table and she'd order tuna tartare.

Millard was one of their own. She came from the old media, not the new media. She had started her career selling ads for *Ladies' Home Journal* and *New York* magazine. Then she became one of Madison Avenue's best-placed insiders as the publisher of *Adweek* and the cofounder of *Brandweek* and *Mediaweek*. "I was paid to have breakfast, lunch, and dinner with the industry," she says. When she was named publisher of *Family Circle* in 1993 at age thirty-eight, she became the first woman ever to run one of the major women's magazines, which, shockingly, had always been managed by men.

In 1996, at forty-one, she was deciding between rival offers to run conventional ad agencies when she was recruited to lead the sales effort at DoubleClick, a startup that was pioneering advertising on the Internet. "I'm too old, I'm overdressed, and I can't work with geeks," she thought. "But I became absolutely fascinated by the idea that for the first time in fifty years, since the birth of TV, we had a new medium. I didn't understand how the pipes worked, but I wanted to be there at the beginning of a new medium."

When Yahoo's top executives recruited Millard in late 2001 to reorganize and run their North American sales force, she knew they needed an attitude adjustment. "I had already spent twenty years in the media business, and it was very frustrating to listen to twentysomethings talk to marketers with disdain," she says. "The Internet industry was leading to its own demise. You have to embrace, not oppose, the industry to lead to change. People aren't going to listen to you unless you're part of their world and you appreciate it."

Millard instilled a new sense of humility and customer service in Yahoo's sales force. She was well connected to the pooh-bahs of branding and advertising and set out to help them understand and embrace the new medium and realize its potential. Millard's changes won over big ad buyers such as Jeff Bell, the vice president of marketing for Chrysler's Dodge and Jeep divisions, who recalls,

"Yahoo was one of the first companies to say, 'We were so arrogant in the dot-com era. We're repentant. Let's say we're sorry and begin to change immediately.' Yahoo was willing to listen to us. That sense of humility and service was good."

Yahoo was no longer trying to revolt against the establishment. It was fomenting revolution from within. Thanks to Millard's insider's understanding of the New York media scene and her formidable energy, she was able to get Madison Avenue to see Yahoo not as an arrogant upstart but as a potential savior that could rescue it from the long, harrowing decline of broadcast television.

By 2005, Yahoo had signed up seventy of America's one hundred largest advertisers, and ads on Yahoo's home page cost as much as $1 million and reached millions of people daily.

•

One of Millard's biggest challenges was that the creative directors—the people who conceived of, wrote, and directed ads—didn't want to waste their talent on the Internet, and for very good reasons: Television was a terrific outlet for their creativity, and they could win prestigious awards for television ads. Online advertising was still primitive and had no prestige at all.

Jerry Shereshewsky, a veteran adman whom Millard hired as Yahoo's ambassador to Madison Avenue, says, "Wenda and I shared a belief that online creative sucked." He had an idea for improving the quality: They would sponsor awards for outstanding creative work in the new medium. The winners received replicas of the over-sized purple armchair from the lobby of Yahoo's headquarters, the Yahoo Big Idea Chair. Before long the chairs became prestige items that people wanted to have on display at ad agency offices. People wanted to win the chairs.

KEY #2
Repeat

The new relationship with Millard and the community she pulled together helped the ad executives develop the new skills they needed for the new medium.

●

Yahoo began hosting educational summits, where the creative directors from different ad agencies could share ideas about innovative practices and how to make the medium more expressive. Yahoo wasn't lecturing them. Yahoo was just the host. The guests were showing off their own work and serving as sources of knowledge and inspiration for each other. Just as Delancey Street provided an environment where ex-cons who had changed could influence other ex-cons, Yahoo created a forum where ad execs who had embraced the Internet could influence their own professional peers.

The summits attracted attendees such as Woody Woodruff, the creative director at Marsteller. "I've been doing advertising for thirty years," he says. "The Internet is not something you instinctively know how to use. Yahoo's creative summits tell us what can be done. These seminars and awards shows are responsible for getting people interested in online advertising. They won't tell you to advertise on Yahoo. They hardly even mention Yahoo." For his own part, Woodruff wound up leading the creation of an interactive campaign to educate consumers about the newly redesigned twenty-dollar bill issued by the Treasury Department. The ads won his agency a Yahoo Big Idea Chair.

At one of the summit meetings in Manhattan in October 2004, Millard and Shereshewsky brought in creative teams to show off four campaigns that had incorporated online advertising in innovative ways. To promote Axe, a deodorant body spray for teenage boys and young men, Unilever produced two comical mock home movies showing women who just couldn't keep their hands off men who used the product. The films attracted 1.7 million visitors to Axe's website in three and a half months.

The summit continued with a presentation about an American Express campaign that created two *webisodes*—five-minute films that debuted on the Web—starring Jerry Seinfeld and his buddy Superman. A daylong set of ads on Yahoo's home page brought several hundred thousand people to Amex's website within twenty-four hours to view the films. More than three million visitors came to the site in two months. By offering an easy tool for people to send e-mails to friends telling them about the films, Amex captured the names and e-mail addresses of 250,000 people—five times as many as it had hoped to get.

The Amex campaign was impressive, but the 165 audience members at the Yahoo summit voted to award the Yahoo Big Idea Chair to Audi for its David Bowie contest. Audi's website let visitors take away two of their favorite Bowie songs and mash them together to create a new song. Then the fans voted for the finalists and Bowie himself picked the winner. Once people came to the website, Audi tracked thousands who configured designs for its cars, sent them to local dealers, and followed through with car purchases, resulting in a 1,032 percent return on investment for the campaign.

KEY #3
Reframe

Learning and mastering the new skills enables ad executives to shift to a new way of thinking about the new medium.

•

The attendees at Yahoo's summit in October 2004 included influential figures such as Ty Montague, who was then the cocreative director of Wieden+Kennedy's New York office, which had already won three Yahoo Big Idea Chairs for its pioneering interactive work, including its Beta 7 campaign—a mock blog supposedly posted by a pre-release tester of Sega's ESPN NFL Football video game. The anonymous tester criticized the game for being so violent that it made him black out and tackle people in real life. The site had 2.2 million visitors in four months.

"The creative departments at ad agencies still see TV as the sexy medium," Montague told me that afternoon at the Yahoo conference, "but their days are numbered. These people will either get religion or get left behind."

Half a century earlier, many ad executives had refused to change too. In the late fifties and early sixties, even after broadcast television came to more than half of U.S. households, the reputable creative directors refused to make television commercials, which weren't very good yet and still weren't admired or respected as an art form. Eventually, they got religion, or got left behind.

For his own part, Montague's success from "getting religion" enabled him to catapult even higher—he became the cohead of JWT, one of the industry's largest agencies. His hiring was a clear symbol that Madison Avenue's power brokers were finally beginning to think within a new frame.

CONCLUSION
Change and Thrive

By 2003, forty-eight-year-old French native Daniel Boulud had established himself as one of the most successful chefs in the world. He owned three restaurants in Manhattan. Restaurant Daniel, his flagship on Park Avenue, received four stars from the *New York Times,* its highest rating, which was seldom awarded. For two consecutive years, the restaurant had ranked number one in the city according to the annual *Zagat's* survey of thousands of frequent diners. And *Bon Apetit* named Boulud "Chef of the Year."

The cooks who worked in Boulud's kitchens came from all over Europe, Latin America, and Asia. But the French master chef was particularly impressed by one man from Japan, who handled everything with chopsticks, whether the food was extremely thin and delicate (a sliver of herbs) or large and unwieldy (an entire lobster tail). Given Boulud's classic French training, the chopsticks techniques looked "strange," he said, but they were remarkably fast. What's more, this Japanese cook could slice food with the "greatest precision" that Boulud had ever seen, even though Boulud himself had apprenticed at some of France's best restaurants. The Japanese man could do it blindfolded. "I learned that there is more than one way to do things right in the kitchen," Boulud wrote in his *Letter to a Young Chef.*

Another surprising incident happened one day when Boulud was walking around Greenwich Village. As he looked through the glass of a storefront, he saw a guy making pizza: "spinning the dough, tossing it in the air, stretching it into a neat circle." Watching the scene, Boulud thought, "He's perfect. I love it. I wish I knew how to do that," he says. "Yet I also knew that to be in the same league I would have to spend at least a year at it."

Boulud has the attitude that we all need to have concerning change.

Think about it: Here's one of New York City's culinary heroes, a celebrity, a man who's wealthy and has scores of people working for him, and he's looking with admiration, delight, and envy at the skills of some anonymous guy who probably makes minimum wage doing what literally thousands of other anonymous guys do every day throughout the five boroughs of the city. And Boulud appreciates how much time and dedication it would take to develop those skills. He's also learning new ways of thinking about his craft from his own *underlings,* who've come from around the globe to learn *from him.* Surveying his kitchens, with their sous-chefs and apprentice cooks from China, Japan, Mexico, Brazil, Israel, and Spain as well as from as his own native land, Boulud thinks: "Every one of them knows something about food in his or her country that none of the rest of us knows." And Boulud realizes that they'll all learn as much or more from one another—by working together, observing, and competing—as they will from a great chef such as himself.

You might say that at this stage of his career Boulud doesn't have to change any longer. He's extraordinarily successful. He's at the very top of his profession. But he got there because of his constant enthusiasm for learning, practicing, and mastering new habits and skills. Boulud was fourteen years old when he began his apprenticeship in a restaurant in Lyon, where he learned to peel vegetables, handle a knife, fillet fish, and pluck the feathers off game birds. He put in the many hard years that it takes to master the difficult and unbending rules of French cuisine, which dictate very particularly how everything should be done, right down to the proper ways to clean a pan or to dice a clove of garlic. And he could have stopped there and worked for the rest of his life as a line cook at a top-ranked French restaurant in Lyon or Paris. But he was able to go much further because he kept learning and mastering the new habits and skills he needed to succeed as a chef (literally the chief of the kitchen), such as how to hire people and get them to work together, and the skills he needed as a restaurateur, such as how to evaluate real estate, raise money, and generate publicity.

Boulud's ultimate success also sprang from his ability to break out of the rigid conceptual framework that he assimilated in his early years. For decades nearly all of the top restaurants in Paris, London, and New York served classic French cuisine. Their long period of dominance had given the French masters a sense of superiority and invulnerability, and those attitudes kept them rigid in their thinking and their ways. But by the time Boulud was emerging as a chef and owner, the culinary ideology was finally changing. In

New York he had to compete with brilliant rivals such as Jean-Georges Vongerichten, who had trained not only in his native France but also throughout Asia and could brilliantly recombine the ingredients, techniques, unique recipes, and distinct mindsets of different traditions. By the time Boulud opened his restaurants, the critics and the customers alike were tiring of the familiarity of French cooking. They expected chefs to excite them with a more global cuisine. If Boulud had stuck rigidly to the tradition he had worked so hard to master, then he never would have served a burger at his French bistro. The burger would never have become one of his most popular and renowned specialties. And if Boulud couldn't break from many years of ingrained habits, he would never have allowed one of his cooks to bring chopsticks into his kitchen. He would have insisted on the classic ways.

Now you might think it unimaginable that a chef like Boulud would have to struggle with the momentous challenges that confront large companies. But try a couple of quick thought experiments: What if all the dairy farmers in the Northeast formed a cartel and enforced an embargo to drive up the price of butter and cream, the backbones of French cuisine, compelling Boulud to rewrite many of his most beloved recipes? Seems unlikely, but then again, no one expected the OPEC nations to embargo crude oil and force General Motors' engineers to learn how to make small cars instead of the hulking gas-guzzlers they loved. The unforeseen events put GM at a severe disadvantage to Japanese rivals that specialized in small fuel-efficient cars.

Here's another hypothetical scenario: What if a new breed of restaurant entrepreneurs could steal away Boulud's customers with fine cuisine that sells for seven dollars a meal instead of the one hundred dollars they routinely pay now? Hard to imagine, but look at what the rival computer makers did to IBM when those upstarts charged $100,000 for computers that could compete with IBM's $4 million machines.

When you're locked into the mindset that helped you succeed, then it's difficult even to think about the profound changes you'll have to respond to. But if you practice change, if you keep up your ability to change, if you use it rather than lose it, then you'll be ready to change whenever you have to. I'd bet that if you forced Daniel Boulud to serve only food that was raw and vegan, he could figure out how to do it and make it delicious. If you told him that he had to prepare a meal for seven dollars, he'd find ways to make it unusually tasty. He's kept changing in his career, so he's remained confident that he can.

What if Boulud decided that he was going to spend a year learning to make pizza? The process could be embarrassing for a man of Boulud's professional stature. The easiest way would be to work as an apprentice to the guy in the storefront pizza parlor in Greenwich Village. But wouldn't the great chef be self-conscious about being seen following orders of a "nobody"? Wouldn't he cringe when the pizzeria customers saw his dough fall to the floor during his early attempts to toss it in the air? What if regular patrons of his upscale restaurants were walking through the Village and recognized him through the storefront glass? It's one thing to make mistakes when you're starting out, but it's very threatening for people who have been accustomed to success for a long time.

Boulud's three restaurants are all located further uptown, so he probably wouldn't have the time to commute downtown to the Village. If he practiced tossing the dough at one of his own restaurant kitchens, he'd subject himself to the possible ridicule of the many people whom he's supposed to inspire and lead. The safest way to learn would be to take a sabbatical and hire the Village guy to teach him in the privacy of his home, but that would mean that Boulud wouldn't be around to run his businesses.

Every aspect of Boulud's success would conspire to make it much more awkward for him to learn new skills or would make it a bigger sacrifice. And yet that's exactly what he has to continue doing if he wants to remain an innovator. Until he had spent a year spinning, tossing, and stretching pizza dough, he wouldn't have a deep understanding of making pizza, and without that insight, he wouldn't be able to master it—or, later, to reinvent it (much as he reinvented the burger by spiking it with expensive black truffles and stuffing its center with the meat of spare ribs slowly braised in red wine).

Now the rest of us might not consider ourselves as skillful or successful in our own fields as Daniel Boulud or, for that matter, the blindfolded cook or even the anonymous pizza guy from Greenwich Village. But we've all been skillful and successful for a long time at many things. Dick Cheney succeeded at hiring and coordinating the work of his many doctors and surgeons, who sustained his health from his first heart attack in his thirties through his White House years in his sixties. People born to the third generation of poverty learned to master the skills necessary for survival in the underclass culture, such as committing acts of violence and crime to gain status within gangs or taking drugs to escape the harshness of their reality. The people at IBM and GM and the mass-marketing companies were all accomplished experts at their fields before those fields changed utterly. And sooner or later that's what always happens. Eventually the world changes, or our solutions are undermined by the problems they create. Even Bill Gates, the most successful capitalist and technologist of his time, found that his success created problems that he was unprepared to face. His power made his company a target for regulators who wanted to break it up, and his wealth exposed him to criticism that he wasn't giving it away and to the challenge of how to give it away without throwing it away.

No matter how successful we are in whatever we do, it's still vital to keep learning—to become successful at something else, something new. And the way to learn is from other people. They have the habits and the skills and the conceptual frameworks that we lack. The trick is learning from them rather than stubbornly believing that our ways are the best ways or the only ways or telling ourselves that we're no longer capable of changing.

If you're going to change, at the very least you need a virtual relationship with a person or community through a book, for example, or a tape recording or a video. Kyle Stewart, the Iowa parole officer, never met the two psychologists who showed him a new way of approaching his work, but he read some of their writings and later watched one of their videotapes. People are often transformed through the inspiration of texts (the Bible, for one) or movies (how many teens have modeled their behavior on screen idols?). Still, it's usually easier to learn when you're together with other people. You wouldn't try to invent your own cuisine if you've never cooked or watched others cooking. At the very least you'd buy a cookbook by a chef you admire and trust. It would be still more helpful to see cooking demonstrations on television or video, and even better if you could enroll in a participatory cooking class with a good teacher.

You would feel encouraged if you could master a satisfying dish within the first few weeks, even if it was a simple one. Later, back at home, you might cook together and share insights and ideas with other friends who are interested in food. If you really wanted to excel at cooking, the best way might be to apprentice in a restaurant and learn from your peers there as well as from the master chef. And if you wanted to master Indian, Thai, or Mexican cuisine, there would be no substitute for traveling and living for a while in one of those countries.

None of these ideas about learning how to cook should be news to any of us. We all know what's involved in the process of learning. We feel motivated by seeing "people like us" who are succeeding at new tasks. We know the value of inspiring teachers and enthusiastic mentors. We appreciate the value of hands-on experiential learning, and practice, and repetition, and modeling our own behavior on the examples of our teachers and our peers. The catch is that we need to think of change as learning.

Too often we assume that change is inspired by private, confidential one-on-one conversations. That's how a doctor deals with a patient. That's the model that inspired Sigmund Freud when he was inventing psychoanalysis, and it's had a powerful influence not only on psychological therapies but also on our most basic assumptions about the process of change. In this book I've tried to show that talking is important but so is *doing*—"Change is a verb," as Mimi Silbert says—and that one-on-one relationships can be valuable but so is taking part in a larger group or a public community. While the medical model assumes that people are sick or disabled and need to be cured, the three keys to change assume that people are well or capable but need to learn habits, skills, and mindsets they don't yet have.

A doctor or psychologist might seem like the obvious choices for an expert who can help you to change. But the process of change is paradoxical, and the best choices are usually not the obvious or commonsensical ones. If you believed in Western medicine, would you have thought of hiring a yoga guru to help you overcome a severe case of heart disease? If you were put in charge of one of the world's largest high-technology companies, would you hire a chicken-shack entrepreneur as your chief of strategy and marketing? Would you take Japanese managers who had never worked with unionized, rebellious, or ethnically diverse workers and let them run a plant with a powerful union and an unruly and highly multicultural labor force?

The process of change can be threatening, so it often helps if we learn new skills and mindsets through relationships with people who feel comfortable and familiar because they share our old skills and mindsets. If you've always believed in Western medicine, it might be less threatening to learn yoga and meditation from a Western medical doctor who grew up in Texas, like Dr. Dean Ornish, than from an Eastern swami. If you're a third-generation drug-addicted felon, you might feel more rapport with others like you than with people who've never been poor, tried drugs, or committed crimes. If you're a middle-aged veteran of Madison Avenue, then you'd rather schmooze and do lunch with Wenda Millard than exchange instant messages with some twenty-two-year-old who acts condescending toward you. If you're Bill Gates and you crave the intellectual charge that you get from smart scientists, then those are the ideal people to introduce you to philanthropy. You need good bridges to get from one conceptual framework to the next.

On that note, please allow me to apologize for the title of this book. The phrase *Change or Die* is a message of fear. But I've been trying to show that while fear may be an effective way of arousing emotions, it motivates change for only a brief time and then people go back into denial. So I knew from the start that I would only have your attention and interest for a short while. The fearful connotations of *Change or Die* may have been enough to get you to buy or borrow this book, but I quickly substituted a message about the importance of new hope and new thinking, which is what sustains change. Instead of *Change or Die,* think *Change and Thrive.* The idea isn't to worry that you're going to wind up like Dick Cheney after his fourth heart attack or GM and IBM after they've lost billions of dollars, but rather to imagine being like Daniel Boulud and realizing your own fullest potential because you've always taken delight in watching and learning from others. Think of change as what you do to remain successful and become even more successful, not as what you'll have to do when your success finally runs out.

Dean Ornish discovered that heart patients weren't motivated by the idea that they could live to eighty-six if they changed, not even if they were already eighty-five. They're motivated by knowing that they can enjoy and improve their lives *right now.* That's the attitude that I've tried to convey. I'm not advocating change because it can make your life or organization better at some distant time in the future. I believe that engaging with people and learning new skills and ideas are among the greatest pleasures of *everyday* life. The ideal isn't to be able to make a dramatic comeback from a life-threatening crisis, but rather to walk around and see other people living and working and playing and say to yourself, "That's perfect. I love it. I wish I knew how to do that," and then going out and mastering it and feeling the sense of satisfaction and accomplishment and joy of understanding something new about the world.

So, kind reader, that's my parting wish for you: Change and *thrive!*

Frequently Asked Questions

Your theory relies on the notion of ego defenses, which was formulated a century ago by Sigmund Freud and further developed by his daughter Anna Freud. But hasn't Freudian psychoanalysis been largely discredited by scientists in more recent times?

Yes, that's true, much of Freud's thinking hasn't withstood the test of time. But in this case, he was absolutely right. "Though modern psychologists and psychiatrists tend to reject orthodox Freudian theory, many acknowledge that Freud was right about the defense mechanisms of the ego," writes Steven Pinker, who teaches cognitive science at the Massachusetts Institute of Technology. "Any therapist will tell you that people protest too much, deny or repress unpleasant facts, project their flaws onto others, turn their discomfort into abstract intellectual problems, distract themselves with time-consuming activities, and rationalize away their motives."

Pinker writes that there are "tactics of self-deception: They suppress evidence that we are not as beneficent or competent as we would think."

Timothy Wilson, a professor of psychology at the University of Virginia, writes in *Strangers to Ourselves* that "people go to great lengths to view the world in a way that maintains a sense of well-being. We are masterly spin doctors, rationalizers, and justifiers of threatening information." Wilson and his colleague Daniel Gilbert have called this ability the "psychological immune system."

You make some references to Alcoholics Anonymous. What exactly do you think about AA and other twelve-step programs, and how do they fit in to your theory of change?

AA is a terrific program that has benefited countless people and helped them change their lives profoundly. For decades AA has demonstrated the power of community. It's something of a historical accident that we've come to think of mind-changing as a process that takes place in private between a doctor and a patient. Freud copied those elements from the practice of medicine and they've stuck in the popular mind. But forming an emotional relationship with a *community* is also a powerful way of creating change, and AA is perhaps its best-known example. AA also relies on one-on-one mentoring of newer members by veterans who serve as role models. The program shows that people often respond better to help from other people who are like themselves. It shows the value of breaking down the "we/they" division. These same ideas were very effective with the ex-cons at Delancey Street and the auto-workers at Nummi, for example. And the twelve-step process provides useful ways for people to expiate the guilt they feel for past actions and to rewrite their autobiographies in ways that let them move forward.

Of course AA and other twelve-step programs don't work for everyone who's struggling with addictions. We shouldn't expect them to work for everyone. Change is inspired by personal relationships, not created automatically by processes, even processes that have been tested and refined over decades of experience. A lot of people go to twelve-step meetings and don't feel a strong connection with the people there or the ideologies they espouse. A study published by the University of California tracked people who attended at least one AA meeting and found that 6 percent wound up sticking with the program for the longer run and getting and staying sober through it. While some critics use that research to dismiss the effectiveness of AA—saying "only" 6 percent succeed—I think that shows that AA is actually quite effective. That's because close, enduring, enriching relationships are so hard to establish.

Six percent is roughly one out of seventeen. If you dated seventeen people and one of them became your soul mate, you wouldn't complain about it. You would probably conclude that the process of dating works. If one out of the seventeen professors you had in your first two years of college wound up really changing the way that you looked at the world, you would probably say that your education was a very good idea. You would say that the institution of college works. If you found a deep sense of connection at the seventeenth house of worship that you ever set foot inside, your spiritual quest would have been well worth the effort. Change is too personal to ever become a one-size-fits-all process.

AA should be seen as a path that works extremely well for some people but not for everyone. I would encourage anyone starting a twelve-step program to shop around awhile for the local meeting that's the best fit. During my obese years I went once to the neighborhood gathering of Overeaters Anonymous. The other participants were all older women with grown children while I was a single man in my thirties. Even though they seemed like warm, compassionate people, I felt that their issues were very different from mine, and I never returned for a second meeting.

I've heard for a long time about the "six stages of change." Do you think that's a valid idea, and if so, then how do the "six stages" fit in with these "three keys."

The "stages" model is very helpful and has been highly influential among professionals in the fields of psychology and health. As set forth in *Changing for Good,* the 1994 book by Drs. James O. Prochaska, John C. Norcross, and Carlo C. DiClemente, it proposes a "trans-theoretical" approach—that is, it looks to all the major schools of psychotherapy for techniques and finds seven that are particularly effective, including "helping relationships" and "emotional arousal." Then it describes the best times to apply each of these techniques during the "six stages of change," from "precontemplation" (a hopeful euphemism for the time when people don't believe that they can change) to "termination" (when the change has become complete and permanent).

The "stages" model has created a clear framework for understanding change that's proven easy to grasp and remember. It has also helped spread many of the most useful insights of psychology to countless people and done incalculable good. I have one very important gripe with it, though. *Change or Die* is focused on the predicament of those "pre-contemplators," whom the stages authors identify as people who are demoralized or who are shielding themselves through psychological self-defense mechanisms such as denial, projection, and rationalization. But it's hard to figure out why the first strategy that the stages authors recommend is "consciousness-raising." They write: "The first step in fostering intentional change is to become conscious of the self-defeating defenses that get in our way. Knowledge is power. Freud was the first to recognize that to overcome our compulsions we must begin by analyzing our resistance to change. We must acknowledge our defenses before we can defeat or circumvent them."

I disagree strongly with this prescription. It rarely does any good to tell someone, "Dude, you're in denial." The facts won't set them free. Knowledge isn't power when the facts are too much to bear. Then knowledge is anxiety. "Pre-contemplators" don't need someone to tell them the truth. They can't handle the truth. That's why they're in denial. Or, as Dr. Jennifer Melfi, the fictional psychiatrist on television's *The Sopranos,* says about her clients: "They lie to me, they lie to themselves."

The point of *Change or Die* is to show how people can change when the facts and fear haven't motivated them. The real key is to give people hope, not facts.

I've read a lot about some of the newer strands of scientific thought, such as evolutionary psychology and behavioral genetics. These theories seem to propose that our ability to change is much more sharply limited than you assert. How do you respond?

These emerging fields of study are full of insights that are fascinating but easily misinterpreted. It's rarely a valid excuse to say that "the caveman in me made me do it" or "my genes made me do it." Even though the lagging nature of evolution may have left you with some of the desires of a caveman while you're living in the world of the microchip, that doesn't mean that you can't give up eating meat when you're in a Dean Ornish program.

And even though scientists have made tremendous accomplishments in the study of genetics, their work hasn't done much to simplify the inherently complicated topic of psychology. Human behavior is an incredibly complex phenomenon, and unlike the color of your eyes, it isn't predetermined by a bit of DNA here or there. We naturally yearn to pick up the science section of the newspaper and learn that they've discovered the gene for fill-in-the-blank, and that's starting to happen, but *not* for the mysteries and intricacies of human action. For example, if both parents come from Eastern European Jewish backgrounds, scientists can run a genetic test to tell whether their child will get certain obscure illnesses that have been passed on within their ethnic group. There are genes for those diseases. But there isn't a gene that has already written the kid's biography. That's a matter of lots of genes and plenty of chance and the powerful influences of community and culture and the curious phenomena known as free will and choice and the awesome power of the human brain to learn and change. And it's all those other factors that help explain why Mimi Silbert and Delancey Street can take people who were supposedly "born psychopaths" and turn them into peaceful, moral individuals who care deeply for others.

You say that crisis doesn't lead to change, but I've heard for a long time about the "burning platform" theory, which says that crisis is indeed what creates change. What's up?

The "burning platform" story has been popular among business people. The premise is that people who work on offshore oil rigs are trained that they should never jump off the elevated platform, since the waters below are so cold and filled with sharks that they would die from hypothermia if they weren't eaten alive first. The training is very effective. But what happens if the rig catches on fire and is going to explode? Well, they'll take their chances and jump off. The idea is that you need a crisis—a "burning platform"—before people will change their ways.

It's a colorful and engaging anecdote, but I don't think it's a good metaphor. A burning platform isn't a change or die situation. It's a "die or die" situation. Stay on the platform and you'll burn or explode; jump off and you'll freeze to death or become lunch for a shark. It doesn't really matter what you do because you're doomed.

The point of *Change or Die* is that even when we think the situation is hopeless, there's usually a different way, a way out; it's simply that we can't see it because it's outside our conceptual frame or we've stopped trying new solutions because we're demoralized by past failures. The situation seems impossible to us, with our mindsets and skill sets, but other people know how to solve it and they can help. Criminal recidivism seemed like an impossible situation but Mimi Silbert knows how to solve it. Heart patients seemed like a hopeless case but Dean Ornish knows otherwise. The Fremont auto workers were considered unmanageable but Toyota proved that they could be the best in the nation.

The idea of *Change or Die* is that we're often limited by thinking we're in hopeless dilemmas—burn on the platform or swim with the sharks—because we've stopped seeking the people and communities that can teach us the way out.

The supposed lesson of the "burning platform" theory is that even if a company isn't in crisis at the moment, the corporate leader might want to *create* a crisis because that's the only proven way to get people to really change. Hopefully this book has suggested another possibility.

You talk about how to change a company or organization and how to change an industry. What about changing the world? How could you apply this theory to political activism?

You might think that most political activists would have learned the most effective ways of persuading people to support their causes, but that's often not the case. So many political efforts fail because activists make the same mistakes that the rest of us make when we try to get other people to change: We rely on facts and fear. Look, for example, at the environmental movement. It's not enough to give people accurate information about issues such as global warming. Nor is it enough to scare them with visions of environmental catastrophe. The death of the planet is simply too scary for most people to think about for long, so we're likely to shield ourselves from the facts and fear with the psychological self-defense mechanisms of denial, avoidance, and such. That's why our political leaders need to give us a sense of hope—the belief and expectation that their leadership and our own efforts will make a difference. If you're sure that Armageddon is coming soon, then what does it matter if we use up the world's oil? However, if you have real hope that humanity and the planet can survive, maybe you'll choose to drive a more fuel-efficient car, or recycle, or invest in an alternative fuel company, or vote for politicians who support curbs on emissions.

What about drugs? Aren't psychoactive drugs a powerful force for changing how we think, feel, and act, whether they're legal (such as antidepressants) or illegal (LSD)? And if so, then how does that fit in with your theory?

There has been a great deal of fascinating scientific research supporting the idea that the power of psychoactive drugs depends on the "placebo effect." That is, they "work" only when the person taking them believes and expects that they'll work. When LSD was first tested in scientific experiments, the people who took it didn't have fantastic creative or spiritual visions; they simply felt sick. But once the lore and legend of LSD spread through the counterculture, and people believed and expected that "dropping acid" would help them experience fantastic creative or spiritual visions, then that's exactly what happened.

A similar phenomenon takes place with psychoactive prescription drugs such as antidepressants. When these new drugs go through "double blind" testing as part of the government's approval process, some of the patients are given the real drug while others are given placebos (sugar pills). Neither the doctors nor the patients know who's getting what. And it usually turns out that the placebos are almost as effective as the drugs. In trials with an "active placebo," which has noticeable side effects (an important clue to patients that what they're taking must be a "real drug," not a sugar pill), then the difference in effectiveness between placebo and pharmaceutical is usually slight. As long as the patients believe and expect that the pill will work, then simply taking the pill inspires hope.

The basic point is that drugs don't "work" automatically. A crucial reason why drugs help us change how we think and feel is that other people have inspired our hope—our belief and expectation—that they'll work. And that fits right in to the first key to change: "Relate."

"Studies of psychoactive drugs reveal them to be model active placebos, since all of the interesting experiences users report from them, whether positive or negative, seem to be products more of expectation and setting than of pharmacology," writes Dr. Andrew Weil. "People who take psilocybin and LSD sometimes have mystical experiences, but some people also have mystical experiences when they pray, meditate, fast, or suffer severe illness. The experiences of many people who take these drugs are quite devoid of mystical or religious feelings. Therefore, mystical experience looks like a capacity of the human mind rather than the effect of any drug."

What about when you've been making real progress toward a new way of thinking, feeling, and acting but then you "relapse" and revert to your old ways?

Erika Leder, a life coach in San Francisco, has an interesting insight on this issue, which she calls the "Van Ness Avenue example."

When people are new to that city, they don't hesitate to drive their cars on Van Ness Avenue, which looks like it should be a good route. It's a wide thoroughfare that cuts straight through the center of town. It's marked prominently on all the maps. It passes right by a number of places where you'll probably want or need to go at some point, such as City Hall, the opera, the symphony, and one of the biggest multiplex cinemas in the city. But after the first few times you've driven on Van Ness, you realize that it's actually an awful road to take. There's always too much traffic. The lights don't roll. You aren't allowed to make left turns at many intersections. There's a reason why the late Herb Caen, who was the city's famed newspaper columnist, called it "Van Mess Avenue."

So you vow never to drive on Van Ness again. You begin learning and practicing alternative routes for getting around town. But then, one day when you're feeling stressed out, you realize that somehow you've turned on to Van Ness. You're stuck in traffic. You feel like an idiot and you can't understand how you could have turned on to Van Ness.

The lesson is that even while we're creating new "neural pathways," the old ones are still there in our brains. Until the new ones become completely second nature, then stress or fear can make us fall back on the old ones. But it's all right. The next time you can take a new route instead of Van Ness. And then take it again and again. Eventually the new pathway becomes fully "automatic."

Look, for example, at the story of my grandmother, Justine, who grew up in Warsaw before she immigrated to the United States as a teenager. When she was in her eighties, my father was visiting her apartment and discovered the diary that she had kept during her voyage to America and her early days in New York City. It was written in Polish. My father asked her to translate it for him, and she couldn't. After seven decades of living here and speaking English, she could no longer understand her native language. In time, even the most basic ways our brains work can change.

Sources

INTRODUCTION

Author interviews

Robert Hare, Dean Ornish, Mimi Silbert

Books

Frank, Jerome D. and Julia B. Frank, *Persuasion & Healing: A Comparative Study of Psychotherapy* (Baltimore: Johns Hopkins University Press, 1993).

Gardner, Howard, *Changing Minds: The Art and Science of Changing Our Own and Other People's Minds* (Boston: Harvard Business School Press, 2004).

————. *Leading Minds: An Anatomy of Leadership* (New York: HarperCollins, 1996).

Hare, Robert, *Without Conscience* (New York: Pocket, 1995).

Hubble, Mark A., Barry L. Duncan, and Scott D. Miller, *The Heart & Soul of Change: What Works in Therapy* (Washington D.C.: American Psychological Association, 1999).

Ingrassia, Paul and Joseph B. White, *Comeback: The Fall & Rise of the American Automobile Industry* (New York: Simon & Schuster, 1994).

Keller, Maryann, *Rude Awakening: The Rise, Fall, and Struggle for*

Recovery of General Motors (New York: William Morrow and Co., 1989).

Kotter, John P. and Dan S. Cohen, The Heart of Change: Real-Life Stories of How People Change Their Organizations (Boston: Harvard Business School Press, 2002).

Articles

Deutschman, Alan, "Making Change," Fast Company, May 2005.

PART ONE: CHANGE 101

CASE STUDY: HEART PATIENTS

Author's interviews

Edith Mossberg, Walt Mossberg, Dean Ornish, Paul Steiger

Books

Frank and Frank, Persuasion & Healing.

Jamison, Kay Redfield. An Unquiet Mind: A Memoir of Moods and Madness (New York: Vintage, 1995).

Kotter and Cohen, The Heart of Change.

Lakoff, George, Don't Think of an Elephant! (White River Junction, Vermont: Chelsea Green Publishing, 2004).

Laughlin, H. P., The Ego and Its Defenses (New York: Jason Aronson, 1970).

Ornish, Dean, Eat More, Weight Less (New York: Quill, 2001).

———Love and Survival: The Scientific Basis for the Healing Power of Intimacy (New York: Collins, 1999).

Articles and papers

Deutschman, Alan, "The Kingmaker," *Wired,* May 2004.

Markel, Howard, "The Heart of the Matter," *Atlantic Monthly,* June 2004.

Miller, Jonathan, "March of the Conservatives: Penguin Film as Political Fodder," *New York Times,* September 13, 2005.

Ornish, Dean, "Statins and the Soul of Medicine," *American Journal of Cardiology,* June 1, 2002.

————"Avoiding Revascularization with Lifestyle Changes: The Multicenter Lifestyle Demonstration Project," *American Journal of Cardiology,* November 26, 1998.

————Testimony before Labor-HHS Subcommittee Hearing on Preventing Chronic Disease Through Healthy Lifestyle, U.S. Senate Committee on Appropriations, July 15, 2004.

————Testimony before Subcommittee on Labor, Health and Human Species and Education Committee on Appropriations, U.S. Senate Hearing on Complementary, Alternative, and Mind/Body Medicine, March 28, 2000.

Ornish, Dean, et. al., "Improvement in Medical Risk Factors and Quality of Life in Women and Men with Coronary Artery Disease in the Multicenter Lifestyle Demonstration Project," *American Journal of Cardiology,* June 1, 2003.

————"Effects of Stress Management Training and Dietary Changes in Treating Ischemic Heart Disease," *Journal of the American Medical Association,* January 7, 1983.

————"Can Lifestyle Changes Reverse Coronary Heart Disease?" *Lancet,* July 21, 1990.

————"Intensive Lifestyle Changes for Reversal of Coronary Heart

Disease," *Journal of the American Medical Association,* December 16, 1998.

Roberts, William Clifford, "Dean Ornish, MD: A Conversation with the Editor," *American Journal of Cardiology,* August 1, 2002.

Waring, Nancy, "Dr. Dean Ornish's Low-Tech Approach to CAD," *Hippocrates,* January 2001.

Websites

Wade M. Aubrey, "Dean Ornish, MD, on CHD Diet and Treatment," published by San Francisco Medical Society, www.sfms.org

Dennis Hughes, "Interview with Dr. Dean Ornish," at www.shareguide.com

www.Harrisinteractive.com for the Harris Poll results.

www.Mori.com for the MORI poll results.

CASE STUDY: CRIMINALS

Author's interviews

Jeff Bezos, David Risher, Mimi Silbert, Kyle Stewart

Books

Bruner, Jacob, *Making Stories: Law, Literature, Life* (New York: Farrar, Strauss & Giroux, 2002).

Gardner, *Changing Minds* and *Leading Minds.*

Glauser, Michael J., *The Business of Heart: How Everyday Americans Are Changing the World* (Salt Lake City: Deseret Book Co., 1999).

Miller, William R. and Stephen Rollnick, *Motivational Interviewing: Preparing People for Change* (New York: The Guilford Press, 2002).

Spector, Robert, *Amazon.com: Get Big Fast* (New York: Collins, 2000).

Articles and papers

Cohen, Adam, "Editorial Observer: A Community of Ex-Cons Shows How to Bring Prisoners Back into Society," *New York Times,* January 2, 2004.

Deutschman, Alan, "Inside the Mind of Jeff Bezos," *Fast Company,* August 2004.

Friedman, Andrew, "The Prison That Thinks It's a Kibbutz," *Jerusalem Report,* January 14, 2002.

James, George, "Beyond Redemption?," *New York Times,* September 28, 1997.

Gonnerman, Jennifer, "Life Without Parole?," *New York Times,* May 19, 2002.

Holt, Jim, "Decarcerate?," *New York Times,* August 15, 2004.

Silbert, Mimi, "The Delancey Street Foundation: A 30-Year Overview."

———"Delancey Street Foundation: A Process of Mutual Restitution," originally published in Frank Reissman and Alan Gartner, editors, *Self-Help Revolution* (New York: Human Sciences Press, 1984).

Websites

www.davidmyers.org

CASE STUDY: WORKERS

Author's interviews

Diane Davidson, John Morgan

Books

Ingrassia and White, *Comeback.*

Keller, *Rude Awakening.*

MacGregor, Douglas, *The Human Side of Enterprise: 25th Anniversary Printing* (Boston: McGraw-Hill, 1985).

Maynard, Micheline, *The End of Detroit: How the Big Three Lost Their Grip On the American Car Market* (New York: Doubleday Currency, 2003).

Watts, Steven, *The People's Tycoon* (New York: Knopf, 2005).

Articles

Angrist, Stanley W., "Classless Capitalists," *Forbes,* May 9, 1983.

Brody, Michael, "Toyota Meets U.S. Auto Workers," *Fortune,* July 9, 1984.

Brown, Warren, "Starring Role for U.S. Autos Fades in West," *Washington Post,* December 26, 1982.

Deutschman, Alan, "The Fabric of Creativity," *Fast Company,* September 2004.

Tasini, Jonathan, Maralyn Edid, and John Hoerr, "The GM-Toyota Linkup Could Change the Industry," *BusinessWeek,* December 24, 1984.

PART TWO: CHANGE 102

CHANGING YOUR OWN LIFE

Author's interviews

Claudia Berman, Richard Fisch, Michael Merzenich, Tim O'Mahoney

Books

Fisch, Richard and Karin Schlanger, *Brief Therapy with Intimidating Cases: Changing the Unchangeable* (San Francisco: Josey-Bass, 1999).

Knapp, Caroline, *Drinking: A Love Story* (New York: Dial, 1996).

Watzlawick, Paul, John Weakland, and Richard Fisch, *Change: Principles of Problem Formation and Problem Resolution* (New York: W. W. Norton & Co., 1974).

CHANGING A LOVED ONE

Author's interviews

Bill Gates

Books

Jamison, *An Unquiet Mind.*

Articles

Specter, Michael, "What Money Can Buy," *The New Yorker,* October 24, 2005.

CHANGING YOUR COMPANY, ORGANIZATION, OR SOCIETAL INSTITUTION

Author's interviews

Rod Adkins, Gary Cohen, David Dobson, Brian Doyle, J. Bruce Harreld, Jon Iwata, Caroline Kovac, Michael Wing

Books

Carroll, Paul, *Big Blues: The Unmaking of IBM*. (New York: Crown, 1993).

Gerstner Jr., Louis V., *Who Says Elephants Can't Dance: Inside IBM's Historic Turnaround* (New York: HarperBusiness, 2002).

Kotter and Cohen, *The Heart of Change*.

Articles

Deutschman, Alan, "Building a Better Skunkworks," *Fast Company*, March 2005.

Lohr, Steve, "On the Road with Chairman Lou," *New York Times*, June 26, 1994.

Matthews, Jay, "America's Best Schools?" *Washington Post*, January 17, 2006.

Websites

www.kippschools.org

CHANGING YOUR INDUSTRY

Author's interviews:

Jeff Bell, Nicholas Donatiello, Wenda Harris Millard, Ty Montague, Jerry Shereshewsky, Woody Woodruff

Articles and speeches

Anders, George, "Cleaning Up Brand Clutter," *Fast Company,* December 2001.

Deutschman, Alan, "Commercial Success," *Fast Company,* January 2005.

———"Demographics of Broadcast TV Just Like the Demographics of Smokers," *Wired,* November 1995.

Sealey, Peter, "The Death of Traditional Ad-Supported TV," speech at the Four Seasons Hotel, Toronto, April 20, 2005.

CONCLUSION

Boulud, Daniel, *Letters to a Young Chef* (New York: Basic Books, 2003).

FREQUENTLY ASKED QUESTIONS

Author interviews

Erika Leder

Books

Hubble, Duncan, and Miller, *The Heart & Soul of Change.*

Pinker, Steven, *The Blank Slate: The Modern Denial of Human Nature* (New York: Penguin, 2003).

Prochaska, James O., John C. Norcross, and Carlo DiClemente, *Changing For Good: The Revolutionary Program That Explains The Six Stages of Change and Teaches You How To Free Yourself from Bad Habits* (New York: William Morrow & Co., 1994).

Weil, Andrew T., *Health and Healing: The Philosophy of Integrative Medicine and Optimal Health* (Houghton Mifflin, 2004).

Wilson, Timothy D., *Strangers to Ourselves: Discovering the Adaptive Unconscious* (Cambridge, Mass.: The Belknap Press of Harvard University Press, 2002).

Acknowledgments

This project began as an article for *Fast Company,* and I would like to thank my many colleagues at the magazine for their support and encouragement, especially Lynn Moloney, for bringing me on to the staff; Mark Vamos, for deftly editing the original story; and John Byrne, for putting it on the cover (in boldface type, no less). Thanks to *Fast Company's* readers for inundating me with enthusiastic e-mails, sharing their own stories, and inspiring me to explore the topic further. I'm indebted to Mark for allowing me to take a short leave of absence and for granting permission for this book to draw on my first "Change or Die" article and several other pieces I wrote for the magazine.

Special thanks to the team at HarperCollins, especially Judith Regan for her vision of turning the article into a book, Cal Morgan for his valuable editorial guidance, and Sarah Burningham for her enthusiasm for spreading the word. I'm grateful to Jonathan Pecarsky, Mac Hawkins, and Suzanne Gluck at the William Morris

Agency. This is the third book I've done under Suzanne's expert guidance, and I've learned that her advice is always right.

Many people worked behind-the-scenes to arrange the interviews for this book and served as my guides through the corporate realm—I'm appreciative of all of them, and especially give my thanks to Brian Doyle at IBM, Heidi Cofran at W.L. Gore, and Nissa Anklesaria at Yahoo. I am grateful to everyone who took part in interviews and opened up their lives and organizations, and want especially to mention Delancey Street's Mimi Silbert, who gave generously of her time. Meeting her was a great pleasure and a lasting inspiration.

The idea of community is crucial to this book, and I benefited greatly from being part of two vibrant and supportive communities in San Francisco while working on it. I'm thankful to my friends at Tully's café in Cole Valley for listening to me talk out these ideas and for providing encouragement and expertise—especially Erika Leder for reading several early versions of the manuscript and offering so many insights. And I feel grateful for the camaraderie and advice of my many fellow writers in the Bay Area, especially Tom Barbash and Cathryn Jakobson Ramin.

Special thanks to my in-laws, Ruth and Tim White, for helping me feel at home in Atlanta; my parents, Hal and Elaine Deutschman, for four decades of encouraging my writing; and my wife, Susan White, for *everything*.

Index